The Economic Philosophy of Jesus Christ

vs.

The Religious Philosophy of Karl Marx

ELIZABETH CLARE PROPHET

SUMMIT UNIVERSITY PRESS®
Gardiner, Montana

THE ECONOMIC PHILOSOPHY OF JESUS CHRIST VS. THE RELIGIOUS PHILOSOPHY OF KARL MARX
by Elizabeth Clare Prophet
Copyright © 2019 Summit Publications, Inc.

For information, please contact
Summit University Press, 63 Summit Way, Gardiner, MT 59030-9314, USA.
Tel: 1-800-245-5445 or +1 406-848-9500.
TSLinfo@TSL.org
SummitLighthouse.org

ISBN: 978-1-60988-318-8 (softbound)
ISBN: 978-1-60988-319-5 (eBook)

Image credits:
P. 12: painting by John Trumbull, 1891, United States Capitol; p. 27: The Portable Antiquities Scheme / Wikimedia Commons / CC-BY-2.0; p. 46: Etching by H. Winstanley after G. Reni, 1728, Wellcome Trust / Wikimedia Commons / CC-BY-4.0; p. 60: 19th century fresco, Église Saint-Maximin de Niedernai, Ralph Hammann / Wikimedia Commons / CC-BY-SA-4.0; p. 65: Rdsmith4 / Wikimedia Commons / CC-BY-SA-2.5; p. 93: portrait by Johann Gottlieb Becker, 1768, Schiller-Nationalmuseum, Marbach am Neckar, Germany; p. 94: portrait by Jakob Schlesinger, 1831; p. 98: photograph of Feuerbach in 1866, Bad Goisern Heritage and Landler Museum; p. 103: photograph by John Mayall, International Institute of Social History; p. 115: photograph from 1879, UNESCO; p. 137: photograph by Nadar, New York Public Library; p. 138: photograph by Nadar, c. 1860, Bibliothèque nationale de France.

SUMMIT UNIVERSITY ☙ PRESS®

Contents

Foreword

The economic philosophy of Jesus Christ versus the religious philosophy of Karl Marx? Seldom do we hear it put this way. After all, Jesus Christ is a religious figure, and Karl Marx became famous for his economic and political theories. Aren't we mixing things up a bit?

Elizabeth Clare Prophet begs to differ. In two groundbreaking lectures—the substance of this book—she points out that Jesus Christ promoted a deeply holistic and practical economic philosophy. She also reveals that Marx was far from being the atheist he is commonly believed to be. Rather, he turned his economic theories into a religious doctrine of sorts, to be adhered to as rigorously as devout souls everywhere adhere to the tenets of the major world religions.

From this simple premise flow profound insights into some of the fundamental questions of our time. What is a fair economic system? What are the principles it should be based on? Are Socialism and Communism really the best answer to well-being and social justice for all? Or should we take into account other, more spiritually-oriented principles that make a different case for how to get to a fairer and just world where happiness, creativity and abundance are available to all?

Read these two enlightening lectures and be prepared to have your own beliefs put under a unique microscope. Then decide for yourself what you will do with the explosive information in this book!

THE EDITORS

The Economic Philosophy
of Jesus Christ

The Relationship between Man and God

I would like to go to the very origin of the teachings of Almighty God given to us through our Saviour Jesus Christ on the subject of government and economics. There are parables in the New Testament that are called the Kingdom Parables, which have to do with what the kingdom of God or the kingdom of heaven will be like when it comes into manifestation upon earth. Through these parables, Jesus was preaching a message of the Law of the I AM THAT I AM* and how it applies to the organization of life within the community of the Holy Spirit.

The term that is translated as *church* in the New Testament actually means "community,"† and community means souls who are united in the vibration of the Christ consciousness. Jesus founded that original community upon the Rock of Peter's confession that Jesus Christ himself was indeed the incarnate Word, *the Christ*.[1] Jesus founded his community upon the ability of the disciple to perceive the living Christ. In other words, Jesus was saying, "This community of the Holy Spirit, this kingdom of heaven on earth, cannot be in manifestation anywhere except where the individual is the disciple of Christ, the disciple of the incarnate Word, and will confess

---

* When that LORD God identified himself to Moses, he said, "I AM WHO I AM," (Exod. 3:14) implying "I will be what I will be. I will reveal myself in the outworking of events. I am a person moving with my people, and I reveal myself in the destiny of men and nations."

† The original Greek word is *ekklēsia*, from *ek-*, "out," and *kalein*, "to call." The church is the community of the called-out ones.

that the Word is incarnate in me and in each one who succeeds me as the representative of the Cosmic Christ."

Without that basic disciple relationship, the kingdom of heaven does not manifest. Without the community of the Holy Spirit, which the United States of America is intended to be, there is not the separating out of light from darkness nor is there the slightest capacity of the individual to meet the challenge of Antichrist. Antichrist is all that denies that the Christ is in your temple, all that denies that you, by putting on that consciousness, can become the fullness of the incarnate Word by the process of the path of initiation.

This is not doctrine and dogma. These are the tenets of our faith. This is the contract, or the covenant, whereby Lord Maitreya, the "LORD God" in Eden, established his covenant with his chelas.*

The guru-chela relationship is the only legitimate relationship for life. This at first seems to be a hard saying because so few are ready to be truly the disciples of Christ in the sense that they are willing to take his mantle, to take his cup of sorrows, to take his cross, to take his mission from the beginning unto the ending.

And yet, it is written, "Lo, I am Alpha and Omega, the beginning and the ending"²—the beginning and the ending of the path of initiation and the beginning and ending of the cycles of our own incarnation of the Word. And we cannot have the beginning without the ending nor the ending without the beginning, because it is the serpent swallowing his tail. It is the perpetual motion of the great sphere of cosmic consciousness within. Once you desire to appropriate that sphere of light because you see it has a blessedness and a bliss, you find that you have to accept the whole sphere. And if you do not accept

---

* The story of the Garden of Eden in the Book of Genesis is an allegorical description of the original Fall of man, as well as an account of a specific Mystery School where twin flames had the opportunity to walk the path of initiation under the person of their Guru Lord Maitreya. Genesis describes how because of disobedience to the Word of the Guru, Adam and Eve were expelled from the Mystery School, and their karma and the world became their teacher.

and become the whole sphere, then you find that that sphere within you becomes the judgment whereby the soul itself is cast into outer darkness, outside of the circle of fire, outside of the circle of oneness.

The soul that has gone forth from that hallowed oneness may only become a part of it again if he becomes subject then unto the Guru, the incarnate Word—the individual Christ Self and the one whom God has sent to represent that Christ Self.

God sent his prophet Samuel (an embodiment of the ascended master Saint Germain) to be the intermediary, that presence of the Christ unto the children of Israel. So Samuel stood in the place of the Christ Self of all, and he gave the Word, the prophecy, the rule, and the law, even as he was the interpreter of the law of God handed down from Abraham to Moses and all the way to Samuel's time.

However, when the people demanded a king, God gave them a king, but not without warning them that this would be the beginning of all of their troubles. Because they sought temporal power and authority and they wanted to be like their neighbors, who were the laggard evolutions, they were given a king. And all of the kings that followed, some good and many not so good, became the degeneration of what should have been the intimate relationship of the individual to the LORD God.

Jesus gives us a parable and the understanding of the foundation of the law of government and of the economy. When we study this parable, we will realize that for any economic system to work, it must be based on that original relationship of the individual soul to the Trinity within his own heart and the Trinity within all those who have become one with God.

The Problem of Idealism

Many of us have a great idealism about government and the economy. This makes us susceptible to believing in systems that either do not work or are not in keeping with the very foundation of the teaching and of the Law. This is because we have an incorrect assessment of human nature.

I have found that the more I have moved from theory to practice in economics and politics, as I studied political science, the more I have come to realize that you can have the very best economic system and the best form of government, but if you do not have an individual, a son or a daughter of God who will ensoul virtue and the law of morality and the cosmic honor flame—being dedicated to the Father, the Son, and the Holy Spirit—no system will work. So it is not a question of which *system* will work, but will the *individual* work under the light of the Holy Ghost?

There are many books discussing the pros and cons of Capitalism and Communism and world conditions today. All these books concern themselves a great deal with theory, a great deal with the calamity that is happening, and a great deal with all of the wrongs and injustices and the evils of the various systems. However, none go to the very core of the message of the great Gurus of the ages and interpret that Word as it applies to the present, interpreting by the Holy Ghost the real message of Jesus Christ, of Lord Krishna, of Gautama, of Moses, of Abraham, of Muhammad, and what they were telling us that we would need to know in the hour that has come—the hour when we must meet the Adversary, who is in full force, completely organized and encamped as the enemy of righteousness. Wherever you look, whether in Africa or Asia or Europe or South America or Nicaragua, you find the Adversary in various avenues of life, ready to devour the blossoming Christ consciousness.[3]

In order to understand what is acting today and how the seed of the Serpent began in the mind of one and then the many, it is necessary to put together the pieces of a cosmic jigsaw puzzle whereby we will come to understand the total message of the Great White Brotherhood, the total lie of the fallen ones, and how the individual soul fits between the two and is able to take dominion over the earth. We must stand at that point in time and space which the ascended master El Morya calls the battle line, the line that is drawn between truth and error, between light and darkness.

This is not an absolute line. It is a line that moves because the tide of error or the energy veil rises. The battle line is here. It is in the Middle East. It is in South Africa. It is in Rhodesia. It is in Cambodia.[4] But it is also right within your very own heart.

We have all built upon a wrong foundation. And that wrong foundation is the entire human consciousness itself, the entire human vibration, the method of human reason. Line upon line, precept upon precept, even the most sincere have taken threads of error and woven them with threads of truth.

America is a nation of God-fearing and truth-seeking people. But there are many people in America who have come to conclusions many years ago, some under the influence of their college teachers, some by an incorrect assessment of the outcome of karma. They hold opinions and make value judgments. Unfortunately, the conclusions that have been drawn by many of our leaders are incorrect.

Therefore, today we are very swiftly losing the platform of evolution in many nations of the earth, losing our technology and our resources. Day by day, we arm the enemy that is bent upon the destruction of the light. It is the battle of light and darkness. It is Armageddon.

Breaking the Molds
of Consciousness

I can remember the shock waves that went through my system when the ascended masters showed me for the first time the records of life, the records of truth and consciousness and what is really happening in the world. On many occasions, so dyed within the fabric of my mind were errors that I began to feel myself trembling in the presence of truth. It was my absolute trust in the presence of the ascended masters and their messenger, that enabled me to say, "God, I accept your message and your messenger, and I will consider and take into my being what I am seeing, hearing, and knowing, and I will allow life to prove to me the fullness of that truth."

I can remember a certain occasion when major concepts that I had accepted along the line of religious philosophy and doctrine were pointed out to me as being erroneous. I came to realize that although the doctrine and the dogma I had been fed and accepted as a little child was incorrect, the Spirit of God had never left me, the spirit of truth and of striving. I came to realize that the cosmic consciousness, the joy, and the healings that I had experienced were not because of that erroneous doctrine and dogma but were in spite of it.

In the same way, many wonderful people who love God and the Lord Christ are experiencing the presence of the Holy Spirit *in spite of* an erroneous doctrine and dogma. These people, who love God and his laws and his government, also accept many of the lies of a government and an economic system that are inconsistent with the laws of God. And yet they are still doing good and manifesting good. The good work that people do is often by sheer dint of the force of the Holy Ghost within them, rather than because of the intellect and where the mental body has positioned itself.

So I commend you to the liquid state—the liquid state of the vast ocean of bliss. It is movement. It is the power of the Mother. But above all, the liquid, the water out of which we are fashioned, is something that can be poured into the mold of the image and likeness of God in which we were originally created. We desire to be poured and re-poured into that mold until we are found in the likeness once again of our Creator.

By free will we have poured that liquid into incomplete molds, and therefore we find that now the molds must be broken. This may be painful, as when you break a limb and it must knit together again. That is because of the calcification of many centuries of being in the wrong mold.

But if we are to win the fight and have the victory of the Christ consciousness, we must learn this: that with all of the books that have been written on political science, economics, and religion, all the sermons that have been preached, all the wisdom that so many of our fellow Americans have today, it is the great synthesis of the Holy Ghost and the Mother flame and the Father and the Son that brings to us not merely a philosophy or a doctrine or a dogma, but a plan of action.

Putting all of this together and positioning the soul at the point of reality, we take what all others have seen, and we move with the hosts of the LORD and the armies of heaven.

The Parable of the Talents

As we read Jesus' parable of the talents, let us invoke the Holy
Spirit that we might perceive the interpretation of the Word of
the Lord by that Spirit.

> For the kingdom of heaven is as a man travelling
> into a far country, who called his own servants, and
> delivered unto them his goods. And unto one he gave
> five talents, to another two, and to another one; to
> every man according to his several ability; and straight-
> way took his journey.
>
> Then he that had received the five talents went and
> traded with the same, and made them other five talents.
> And likewise he that had received two, he also gained
> other two. But he that had received one went and
> digged in the earth, and hid his lord's money.
>
> After a long time the lord of those servants cometh,
> and reckoneth with them. And so he that had received
> five talents came and brought other five talents saying,
> Lord, thou deliverest unto me five talents: behold I
> have gained beside them five talents more.
>
> His lord said unto him, Well done, thou good and
> faithful servant: thou hast been faithful over a few
> things, I will make thee ruler over many things: enter
> thou into the joy of thy lord.
>
> He also that had received two talents came and
> said, Lord, thou deliverest unto me two talents: behold,
> I have gained two other talents beside them. His lord
> said unto him, Well done, good and faithful servant;

thou hast been faithful over a few things, I will make thee ruler over many things; enter thou into the joy of thy lord.

Then he which had received the one talent came and said, Lord, I knew thee that thou art an hard man, reaping where thou hast not sown, and gathering where thou hast not strawed: And I was afraid and went and hid thy talent in the earth: lo, there thou hast that is thine.

His lord answered and said unto him, Thou wicked and slothful servant, thou knewest that I reap where I sowed not, and gather where I have not strawed: Thou oughtest therefore to have put my money to the exchangers, and then at my coming I should have received mine own with usury.

Take therefore the talent from him, and give it unto him which hath ten talents. For unto every one that hath shall be given, and he shall have abundance: but from him that hath not shall be taken away even that which he hath. And cast ye the unprofitable servant into outer darkness: there shall be weeping and gnashing of teeth.

—Matthew 25:14–30

In his parables of the kingdom of heaven, Jesus gave us an understanding of the path of initiation according to the seven rays for entering into higher consciousness, the consciousness of the Christ. When he begins this portion of his Olivet discourse with the statement, "For the kingdom of heaven is as," he is saying, "Higher consciousness, the consciousness of spirit, may be attained in the following manner."

In the case of this parable, Jesus gives us the teaching for the attainment of higher consciousness in the economies of the nations. In fact, the parable of the talents sets forth the science and the religion of the abundant life in its practical application to the economies of the nations.

The Declaration of Independence, by John Trumbull.
Each century of America's history from its founding as a nation represents a new phase of spiritual evolution. The first century was the initiation of the Father principle, the power of the first ray. The second century was the energy of the Son, the wisdom ray. In its third century, which began in 1976, America faces the initiation of the Holy Spirit, the need to infuse divine love into all that has been built in politics, economics, religion, and education.

We are contemplating the first two hundred years of America's destiny as the outpicturing of the light of the Father and of the Son, the power and the wisdom. As we have begun in 1976 the third century of America's history, that century represents the initiation of love, of the Holy Ghost, and nowhere is this initiation more important than in the foundation of the flow of that love as supply.

The entire momentum of Antichrist bent on death, not life, and upon the destruction of the soul before it fulfills the full potential of the Christ, is directed at the economies and the governments of the nations. Jesus taught this. That is why he says, "The kingdom of heaven is like unto ...," then gives a parable. The correct unlocking of that parable by the Holy Ghost gives us a plan, a direction, a matrix for a certain part of life and how it should be lived—how government, the economy, religion, education, and science should be in the true relationship of man to God.

Yin and Yang

Today there are two systems vying for allegiance East and West. One is Capitalism. The other is called Communism, or Socialism. Neither of these is new. These two principles have existed side by side since the very incarnation of the Word and since the first rebellion against that Word.

The problems of East and West are merely the problem of the equation of the Alpha to Omega exchange of energy upon the planetary body, the yin and the yang. The problems of East and West have to do with the harmonization of the Father-Mother principles within the individual and within all people. Unfortunately, the harmony of the Father-Mother God, of Alpha and Omega, has been misconstrued into all types of concepts of good and evil, or the "haves" and the "have-nots."

We have a right to the divine economy and to experience its full expression upon earth. We look then to the resolution of the question: What is the divine economy and what is its foundation? The answer to that question actually becomes the eye in the capstone of our own pyramid of life and the pyramid of life of the nation.

The Great Seal of the United States of America has within it the eye in the capstone waiting to be placed upon the foundation that we build as a nation—a foundation to be built upon the Father, the Son, and the Holy Spirit in three centuries of a path of initiation. Our path of initiation as sons and daughters of God seems to have come to an absolute standstill because we as a group, as a nation, have not been able to meet the challenges of the sacred fire of the Holy Spirit.

The Great Seal of the United States. The eye within the capstone is the All-Seeing Eye of God and represents the third-eye chakra. The crown chakra at the apex of the capstone marks the point through which we pass to unite with God. The capstone has not yet been placed, symbolizing that the work of building the nation is not complete.

The resolution of the problems of the economy is actually the placing of the eye in the capstone upon the pyramid. It is the raising up of the energy of the Mother flame from the base to the crown to the third-eye chakra. It is the centering of the oneness of the Law within that center. So the image tells us that without initiates of the sacred fire, without sons and daughters of God on the path of initiation, this nation and any nation cannot truly solve the question of the abundant life or of economics.

The very urgent need of the hour is the resolution of the problem of the economy, and yet we find that the path of initiation is wanting in our leaders and in those who are in control of the economy. Therefore the Great White Brotherhood addresses the question of Capitalism versus Communism, the uses and abuses of both systems, and sets forth solutions that are both practical and spiritual for the unfoldment of the potential of the soul within the family, the community, and the nation, and then within the family of nations.

The teachings of Jesus Christ cover every subject, every phase of human evolution. They have been grossly misunderstood and misapplied and even abused by the fallen ones who have quoted scripture. However, it is impossible to understand the scripture or the great mysteries of the kingdom that he taught except by the gift of the Holy Spirit.

Unfortunately, many of those who are the followers of

Christ today, who should have the fullness of the Holy Spirit and should comprehend these very statements, are positioned in rebellion against the very teachings which Jesus Christ gave. They proclaim a gospel that says religion should be kept out of politics and economics. That is the original lie of the Serpent himself.

The Rock of Christ

Without the Holy Spirit, we do not understand the foundation of the City Foursquare, which the Lord Christ has laid. The City Foursquare is the Matter plane.[5] It's where we are—this temple, this city, this nation. Wherever you are, the Matter plane is your challenge. The problem is that we do not understand Jesus' coming as having provided the children of light with the means to take dominion over the earth, with the economy and the government squarely upon the shoulders of the Lord Christ.*

The government and the economy cannot be upon the shoulders of a fictitious Jesus who is always coming but never arrives. He's always going to come and save the world, but somehow he never gets here. And so we preach our sermons and hear them year in, year out, of submission to the fallen ones upon the planetary body until the time of Jesus' coming. Well, if we wait much longer, we will find that there will be no place for him to come to.

The real place of his coming is in the temple of man. And the government and the economy that must be upon his shoulders must be upon his shoulders *now*, within *you*. It must be upon the shoulders of the Christ, who now comes into your temple because you submit unto him and confess that he is the Lord of your temple and the Lord of the nations.

The Second Coming of Jesus Christ is the moment you

---

* "For unto us a child is born, unto us a son is given: and the government shall be upon his shoulder: and his name shall be called Wonderful, Counsellor, The mighty God, The everlasting Father, The Prince of Peace" (Isa. 9:6).

accept that the Christ that was in Jesus is the same Christ that is in you. And the consequence of that manifestation of faith is the transformation whereby you become a new creature and you go forth to take dominion in the economy and in the government.

If all of the free people of the world and all of the lightbearers of the world who have had a conversion to Jesus Christ would accept this one principle, that the government shall be upon his shoulders within them, they would rise and take dominion and we would see the overthrow of the fallen ones in Capitalism and in Communism and in every nation. We would see the overthrow of the carnal mind within our own temple. We would see the slaying of that carnal mind by the Christ whom we have become.

When that message is spoken again and again, it must never seem repetitive, because until it is spoken, until we have become it, until it has been transferred and translated by the Holy Ghost, by the only flame by which it can be translated, then we may be hearers of the Word but not doers of the Word,[6] and therefore we will not be found worthy in the judgment.

That same principle must be applied to every area of involvement of the lightbearer. No matter what your job, your profession, your calling, your occupation, the government, the God-control of that energy is upon the shoulders of the Christ in you when you allow it, when you decree it, when you become it, when you use the violet flame.*

The most serious crisis upon us is the manipulation of the money and of the government and economy of this nation for the destruction of our way of life. When you can't buy bread, own a home, or put enough gasoline in your car because of inflation, it's a crisis. When prices are not equal to the flow of

---

* The violet flame is the seventh-ray aspect of the Holy Spirit, a spiritual flame of joy, freedom, and transmutation. It is used to change negative energy into positive energy, including the transmutation of negative karma. It is invoked in meditation and most powerfully using decrees, affirmations, and mantras according to the science of the spoken Word. For more information, see www.violetflame.com.

energy of the sacred labor, then the fallen ones have succeeded in destroying the light of the Christ in the individual and in the nations.

We are upon the brink of that catastrophe. The ascended masters have told us that the only reason that economic collapse has not come has been the staying action of the LORD God through the hand of the chela through the science of the spoken Word.

When we understand this parable of the talents, that wisdom becomes a Rock. Then when we go through that turmoil and turbulence of doubt and fear and the pressures of the end justifying the means, or the frantic wave of the mass consciousness reacting in fear because its security has been taken from it, we will be able to stand upon the Rock of divine understanding, the Rock of the Word. We will know those threads of truth and error. Therefore we will not succumb when the Serpent enters the Garden and gives us the temptation that we all must face. We will be able to conquer the Eve within us, conquer the submission of the divine woman unto the carnal mind.

And so rather than point the finger at Eve as the one who succumbed to the logic of the Serpent, let us examine his logic. Let us examine the logic of the Lord Christ, and let us know that under the pressure of desire, under the pressure of human need, we will not give in to the alternative to the teachings of the Lord Christ and Lord Maitreya, which were presented many thousands of years before Jesus gave this parable.

The True Foundation
of the Abundant Life

*For the kingdom of heaven is as a man travelling into a
far country, who called his own servants, and delivered
unto them his goods.*

The term *the kingdom of heaven* means "the consciousness of
spirit," the plane of higher consciousness, which is the origin of
our own individual Christ Self awareness. It is the plane of First
Cause, the cause behind the effect of the Matter plane. The
kingdom of heaven is the point of beginning, the point of
origin.

We must rise to that higher consciousness through the
nexus, who is Christ, to the plane of First Cause. There and
only there can we be in control. This gives us dominion of fire,
air, water, and earth from the center, the white-fire core of
being, Spirit.

It is from that point of reference, from the fiery core of
Alpha and Omega, that the man travels into a far country. He
descends from the plane of higher consciousness into the plane
of Matter. This is the story of the incarnation of every soul.

In this reference point, the man calls his servants unto him
and delivers unto them "his goods." We see then that there is a
hierarchical order or scheme of things in the universe wherein
the individual who has the greatest attainment in higher consciousness holds the key to the kingdom of heaven or the
consciousness of Spirit. The goods which he delivers are the
portion of his higher consciousness that he gives to his servants,

his disciples. He gives them an increment of light.

This teaches us that the path of initiation, the increase of light, is for one purpose. It is to impart that light to those of lesser light. That is the supreme obligation of the order of hierarchy. The light is not a gift; it is a loan. What the servants do with the light will determine whether they will be able to keep the original investment and/or a portion of that which they have multiplied, depending upon the contract that is made with the man—and the man in this case is the God-man, the Guru.

The fullness of that contract does not happen to be mentioned in this parable, but the giving of light from the master to the servant is always based on a contract, an agreement based on the laws of God and man's keeping of those laws. The person of lesser attainment is always the servant of the one of greater attainment.

These points of the law have been challenged vociferously within the governments and the economies of the nations. An order of hierarchy is a principle of the Christ against which revolutionaries have rebelled for hundreds of years. The idea that there could be a hierarchy or there could be individuals holding greater light than others is an anathema to the rebels. It's a cause for outrage among precisely those individuals who do not have attainment and therefore fall into the servant class. These individuals who have rebelled against God and the Lord Christ are the original rebellious ones, the fallen ones.

The world is filled with people who will not submit themselves to the law of the Christ. Here it is set forth: The kingdom of heaven, the consciousness of Spirit as it applies to the economies of the nations, is as a man traveling to a far country. He takes this long journey, and he goes from Spirit to Matter. He meets with those who are beneath him in vibration and imparts to them an increment of light, because only by imparting to them an increment of light can they be elevated to his plane. But he will exact from them something in return.

Nowhere in the universe can you get something for

nothing. But this law has been violated in the Socialistic and Communistic doctrines of this century and of all past centuries.

This guru-chela relationship is the foundation of the abundant life. It is by no means impractical. It is the most practical order of life upon earth. It is the easiest, most joyous, most happy life when we have ourselves in alignment with the inner Christ and with the living Christ. All else is hard work and the suffering of outer darkness.

It seems that the world today has not learned that lesson, and even on the very brink of its own self-destruction, it will never say die. It does not confess the name of the Lord and recognize that to confess that he is Lord means that he must be Lord in this temple where I stand, where you stand. Where you declare that he is Lord, you must acknowledge that Christ is come in that place.

When this relationship is departed from, when we ignore the great Gurus of the ages and their teachings, all of civilization, all of life breaks down. Over and over and over again, continents have sunk, civilizations have fallen, cataclysm has come because of the ignoring of the great avatars of the ages of East and West—not so much by the children of God, but by the fallen ones who come and lead the children of God astray.

When we depart from a hierarchical order where those who have greater ability and talent are fit to rule over those of lesser ability and talent, we enter into that state of anarchy, of chaos and confusion which is referred to by Jesus Christ as "outer darkness." It is the rebellion of the fallen ones who will say, "We will not come under the yoke of the servant sons of God."

Jesus said, "My burden is light, my yoke is easy."[7] *Yoke* is the term for karma. So Jesus is saying, "My karma is easy. The way that I show you to balance your karma is by the sacred fire of the Holy Ghost. If you will accept *my* yoke, which is the yoke of the guru-chela relationship, even though you may have to perform those works that appear subservient, your soul will be free. Your soul will be gaining its immortal birthright."

What appears to be slavery to those who are in rebellion against the love of God is actually the most intimate, loving relationship that could ever be enjoyed by any person anywhere. It is oneness with Jesus Christ. And in that oneness, no labor, nothing that is required of us is too much.

Because all that we do is so infused with his light, there is no task too difficult, too unpleasant, too lowly for us. We understand that he is taking us through these tasks for the establishment of humility, for the restoration of innocence, so that we can finally be crowned with the crown of life and receive the power that the fallen ones seek to gain by illegitimate means.

Spiritual Economics

All of us who are living on planet Earth in this hour have already received our talents, our portion of the abundant life, both through the genius and talent conveyed through our genes and chromosomes and through the abundant natural resources of our environment. What we have done and what we will do with these resources will determine whether or not we pass our initiations on the path of Christhood.

These initiations do not come because we leave the world of economics. They come within that world. And therefore we are required to master our economics. Economics is just not money. Economics is the supply and demand of the energies of our personal karma. Economics is how the balance of light and darkness measures in our world.

How much money do you have in the bank? How much light is in your causal body? How much can you expend on an investment to bring Christ consciousness to the millions? How much are you in debt to the law? And how much does that debt affect your ability to become a world server?

This is economics. This is the abundant life. If you can't be a world teacher or a world server because of this, that, or the next thing such as the karma or the economics of your family, this is only an outer manifestation of the inner fact that your karma itself, your failure to resolve your debts to God, has made you such a debtor that he cannot give you more light in order for you to be able to serve.

In that divine economy, it behooves you to come forward and say, "Almighty God, I owe you many debts. I will pay off these debts. I will practice the science of the spoken Word. I will invoke the violet flame. I will transmute this energy, and I will send that energy back to you, back to the great storehouse of the causal body, so that when I desire to go forth as a servant son for the conversion of multitudes, when I desire the gifts of the Holy Spirit, I will have something in my cosmic bank account that you may look upon and say I am a good risk."

This is economics. And it is not removed from the economics of the Federal Reserve System or of our government today. The making of money out of nothing increases the debt of the American people to themselves and to the Federal Reserve. It also decreases the value of the money that they already have.[8]

The devaluation of the dollar in comparison to foreign currencies and within our own nation is simply the manipulation of karma, the manipulation of debt, the manipulation and misuse of God's light that has already been brought upon us by those whom we have allowed to represent us. The gold of the Christ consciousness is no longer a standard in the economy of this nation. The gold of the Christ consciousness reflected in the metal gold should be the Spirit-Matter standard, a pillar of fire into which all other things are placed for transmutation.

The teaching of economics cannot be divorced from the principles of the alchemy of the Father, the Son, and the Holy Spirit. We are all debtors to life. To be the fullness of the servant son to meet the needs of the nations, to meet the needs of the community of the Holy Spirit, we must have a very intense desire to pay that debt. Most God-fearing people are very concerned when they owe money. They like to have all their bills paid on time and ahead of time. People who are not God-fearing sometimes like to get away with not paying their bills.

Those who are totally irresponsible and who squander God's energy, whether by ignorance, by malice, or by the intent

The framers of the US Constitution provided for a monetary system based strictly on gold and silver. Article I, Section 10, reads, "No State Shall ... make any Thing but gold and silver Coin a Tender in Payment of Debts." The abandoning of a gold standard removed any limits on the Central Bank's ability to manipulate the money supply and the economy. Even more than this, it removed gold from its intended role in the spiritual and material regulation of the economy.

to manipulate life, are always the ones who say, "Gimme more, gimme more." They want more light, they want more initiations, they want to get the energy of the altar, and they want to have what they consider other people have that should really belong to them.

This affects our money system, but it is not confined to money. It affects our values. It affects society. Money is only one end of the spectrum. The economics of money in this nation is only one part of the vast interchange of life and of energy. As you are balancing your debts to life, you have an opportunity to become a servant son.

The Servants
and Their Talents

And unto one he gave five talents, to another two, and to another one; to every man according to his several ability;...

To one servant the Guru gives five talents, to another two and to another one. Each one is given the opportunity to multiply a portion of the higher consciousness of the Guru. The higher meaning of the talent is that it is an increment of the Christ consciousness. It could be your ability as a teacher or as a pianist or as a healer or as an organizer or as someone who tends the elementals in the garden. Each of these is a talent, and any talent is a gift on loan.

One of the mistakes we make is to consider that these talents are our own and that we may use them selfishly or not use them for the good of others. If you want to remain within the hallowed circle of God's Being and your relationship to him, you do not have the freewill choice to use a talent selfishly. That is the law. He who violates the law will suffer by that violation.

For this incarnation, God has given certain talents to each one of us in the person of our individual Christ Self. These may not be left idle. They must be multiplied to the glory of God and in the service of Christ for the blessing of humanity, who are the body of God. The talents are represented as a sum of money because Jesus is teaching a parable and money is where the manipulation of the fallen ones is. But the teaching

A Roman silver denarius from the reign of Augustus.
In New Testament times, a talent as a monetary unit was about 80 pounds (36 kg) of silver, 6,000 denarii. One denarius was the usual pay for a day's labor, so a talent was the amount someone could earn in twenty years, the equivalent of about a million dollars today. This parable is the origin of the meaning of *talent* in English to denote a gift, skill, or innate ability.

doesn't apply to just money. It relates to the total equation of consciousness.

In the parable, these talents (a portion of higher consciousness) are given according to the individual's prior demonstration of the law of abundance, which is read in the Bible as "his several ability." What you have done with talents in previous incarnations determines which talents are available to you today. How much light you have multiplied in the past determines how much light you are given to multiply today.

If you don't like your meager portion, you must multiply it 100 percent, and then God will give you a greater portion. So if you don't like what you've got, you must apply the law and you can change: You can change your state. You can change your talents.

The Law of Self-Transcendence

These servants, these chelas, are being tested in the law of self-transcendence, the law of the multiplication by the factors of Alpha and Omega. This is the law that requires that whatever we are, we transcend it.

We must transcend what we are. God will not allow us to become satisfied that now we have attained and become the Christ. No ascended master can be satisfied on a given day with his attainment of the Christ consciousness. And you cannot be satisfied. The law requires multiplication of the self, of one's talents, so that the fruit of those talents should continually bless all life. And when that fruit is partaken of by others, it passes on to them the elements of our own self-mastery and our own initiation.

The fruit of the action of my living is the teaching that I give. If you partake of that fruit, you will become it, assimilate it, and digest it. So the fruit of action, which is always the Holy Spirit, is the means whereby the whole body of God is leavened, is raised.

The whole body of God is in a resurrection spiral because the ones at the top, the sons and daughters of God standing in the position of saviour, guru, avatar, have chosen to multiply their God consciousness, and give of that fruit to their servants, who then multiply the fruit so lesser evolutions can in turn partake of that fruit. This is the responsibility of those of greater attainment. Those of greater attainment always have greater responsibility than those of lesser attainment.

Saint Germain once made a wry comment about people who occupy a narrow band and spectrum of consciousness and who are wholly satisfied with that state of consciousness. Because they may be superior to a circle of four or five people around them, these satisfied ones have no desire to increase. He said, "How shall we tell people of such a nature that they are lacking, when they think that they are the king of the mountain?"

We are being tested daily in the law of self-transcendence. We transcend the self each day by the law of the multiplication of Alpha and Omega, the Father-Mother God. The Father-Mother God in the fiery core of your being is the energy by which the talent is multiplied.

Take a given sum of light, a given sum of energy, a given sacred labor. The increase is the added factor of Alpha and Omega. We know that this is the body and blood of Christ. We know that it is the very essence, Spirit and Matter, of our personal Guru and Saviour, Jesus Christ, of Saint Germain, and of all who have gone before in that same initiation. So the Alpha-Omega, the multiplier, is a principle. But we can't multiply with only a principle. The only way we can multiply a talent is by that principle having become *person* in the hierarch who has preceded us on the Path.

Saint Paul said, "I planted, Apollos watered, but God gave the increase."[9] I may work the Work of God. I may do my best to prepare a manuscript, a publication, or to help with the administration of the organization. That is my planting. The watering of that planting will be the grace of God upon it. But the increase will come through the person of God who has preceded me—through the Guru and through my own personal Christ Self.

These are hard sayings to swallow for those who have rebelled against the law. Accepting them means that you will have to become humble enough to realize that you need your guru, that you need the person on the next rung of the ladder. You need your department head, your supervisor, your employer. You need the one with whom you are sharing a guru-chela relationship in some form.

You may only need that person for a week or a month, but there is a conveyance of consciousness, of talent, of information, of expertise, of technical know-how. And as long as you are in a position of working to attain that level, you are under that individual's Christ Self, even if that person may be very imperfect or very annoying and have seemingly far less outer attainment than you do.

Some people kick over the traces of this guru-chela relationship because they are always waiting for the perfect guru who can measure up to their standards. They forget what El Morya said: "If the messenger be an ant, heed him." Sometimes your messenger, your guru, is the ant that is crawling across the floor that teaches you a very important lesson about your own consciousness.

Hierarchy and Initiation

... and straightway took his journey.

As soon as the Guru has set forth the initiation and given to the three individuals the necessary ingredients of the alchemy, he withdraws and takes his journey. He recedes into higher planes of consciousness.

The absence of the Guru during the period of initiation is essential in the alchemy of self-transcendence. It is the law that we have seen repeated over and over again in the lives of those who have preceded us on the Path. The increment of light is given, the power, the teaching, the love is given, and then the teacher is removed. Now the individual has his free will, and he has time and space in which to demonstrate his initiation.

God gave Adam and Eve the conditions of being within the community called Eden, and then he withdrew. This means that if we are going to become the Guru,* we cannot do so by leaning upon or being dependent upon the aura of the Guru while we are passing the initiation. We have to do it by expanding the flame in our own heart and by meeting the trials and tribulations and testing that come through our own yoke of karma.

There are conditions in Spirit and Matter that must be present for this alchemy of the multiplication of substance: a platform of evolution (the earth body, the state, the nation, the epoch), the individual in physical embodiment, the presence of the guru, the teacher, the presence of energy—in other words,

---

* I.e., pass our initiations so that we, ourselves, rise to that level of attainment

both time and space, the gift of free will and consciousness, and the increment of light.

Think about what it takes for God to bring all of these conditions together so that we may pass one test. We must have an incarnation. We must grow up. We must be educated. We must come through a family. We must be on a planet where there is law and order and government, where there are systems, where there is culture, where there is a tradition of the guru-chela relationship. All of these things must come together so that in any given instant we can say no to the beast of human greed, we can say no to selfishness, we can say no to condemnation. And in saying no, we can put it into the flame and come up higher.

Our gratitude should abound for the fact that here today in the United States of America, all of the necessary conditions are present for us to experience the initiation. We are not missing any of them. We have by the light of the Holy Ghost the very living presence in our midst of the great Gurus—not one, but many ascended masters. Your soul is a free agent operating within the laboratory of consciousness with only the bounds of man's habitation that were set in the beginning by the LORD as our confinement. This earth sphere is our laboratory.

However, through the abuse of time and space and free will, which has resulted in karma (the effects of causes we have set in motion), we now have limiting factors on the Path that are self-imposed. There are the limitations of our decreased lifespan[10] and the limitations resulting from all those things we have done in the past that have brought our nation and our earth to such a precarious position. There is also the limitation of our dharma, which is the divine plan, the duty to realize the fullness of our Real Self and in the process balance our karma. Even when we had no karma, our original dharma was still to fulfill the Real Self. But now our dharma also includes the requirement to balance our karma.

The free will of the individual is expressed through the sacred labor, which is always the action of the hand of God, the Holy Spirit. Through the sacred labor, the soul draws forth its individual genius, and by that genius, by the momentum of prior service, each in his own way multiplies the talents that he is given.

This establishes the foundation for the reward for excellence according to achievement through the freewill expression of individual genius by this sacred labor. The reward for excellence is a condition of the guru-chela relationship. However, we see economic systems today that do not acknowledge that the individual has the right to the reward for excellence.

The Reward for Excellence

After a long time the lord of those servants cometh,
and reckoneth with them. And so he that had received
five talents came and brought other five talents saying,
Lord, thou deliverest unto me five talents: behold I
have gained beside them five talents more.

His lord said unto him, Well done, thou good and
faithful servant: thou hast been faithful over a few
things, I will make thee ruler over many things: enter
thou into the joy of thy lord.

He also that had received two talents came and
said, Lord, thou deliverest unto me two talents: behold,
I have gained two other talents beside them. His lord
said unto him, Well done, good and faithful servant;
thou hast been faithful over a few things, I will make
thee ruler over many things; enter thou into the joy of
thy lord.

It is written in the parable that after a long time the lord of
those servants, the Guru of the chelas, returns to reckon with
them to see what they have made of their period of aloneness.
They have received the light of the guru; they must now give an
accounting.

"What have you done with my light? What have you done
with my higher consciousness? What have you done with the
energy that is God's? How have you manifested in the Matter
plane that which has come forth from the original blueprint of
the Spirit plane?"

The first servant, who received five talents, multiplied them 100 percent, and he presents his lord with ten talents. This is the requirement of the law; the chela must manifest an equal measure in the Matter plane of that which he has gained from Spirit. That seems a hard saying. But that is the price we pay for the gift of the presence of the Brotherhood.

The masters haven't stated a time limitation. We expect to go on evolving for hundreds and thousands of years. But ultimately the light we are given must be multiplied 100 percent. An increase of two or three or four talents for the five would not have fulfilled the law.

Likewise, the servant who was given two talents returns them with two more. He has duplicated his Guru in the Matter plane. The Guru has taken a portion of Spirit, placed it in the care of his servant in Matter, and in Matter the servant has doubled it. So now he gives the talents back to the Guru. He keeps the increment of light of the Guru that he himself has become. He has transcended himself. He has fulfilled the law of self-transcendence through the Mediator, the person of the Christ, the Guru. He has duplicated the Spirit consciousness of the Guru, and in that virtue, in that particular aspect of genius, he has in fact put on the Guru's consciousness.

Both of these individuals receive the very same commendation. Although it may seem redundant, the words are repeated in the Bible because they illustrate a very important law: "Well done, thou good and faithful servant. Thou hast been faithful over a few things, I will make thee ruler over many things. Enter thou into the joy of thy lord."

This shows that the individuals were not in competition with each other, but were expected only to live up to the fullest potential of their own Christed being. Whatever the level of their own higher consciousness, that ability was matched by the Guru and they were expected to multiply that ability, that talent.

Each one will become a ruler in his own domain according to his own ability. It is clear that the one who has the mastery

of five talents will be in a hierarchical position over the one
who has mastered two talents, yet each one is considered as
having equal opportunity in the sight of God and as having
gained an equal increment of mastery according to the level of
his individual initiation.

Grace and Works

Entering into the joy of the lord is an invitation to enter into the higher consciousness of the Guru as the reward for having been faithful over a few things. One doesn't simply enter into the joy of the lord of oneself. The old argument as to whether we make it by God's grace or by our works is resolved by this point. We must work the works. We must multiply the talents. But unless the Lord Jesus Christ come and stand before us and say, "I will make thee ruler over many things. Enter thou into the joy of the lord," we cannot advance into a higher plane.

The sphere of God consciousness is available only to those who have attained to it by works and by the offering of grace. We may meet all the requirements of the letter, but unless the fullness of the Spirit be present we will not have that acceleration.

In other words, you cannot simply follow doctrine and dogma and then demand that the universe accelerate you or demand that you go to heaven. You cannot make promises to other people that if they follow this doctrine and this dogma that they will attain to the heaven of God's consciousness. This is not enough. They must be disciples of the Christ. They must be chelas of the Guru. And by that tie to hierarchy, it is the option of God to give the increase.

He gives it. We don't earn it. We may think we're earning it. But if we think we're earning it, if we think we have a right to it, then we enter into that state known as spiritual pride, where we think we can come and go out of the spheres of God's consciousness at will.

The ones who have taken the left-handed path, as Jesus said, are those who seek to take heaven by force.[11] They try to force the energies of God, and they think that they do so when they increase the energies of the chakras within their own temple. But in fact when they do this, the entire realm of Spirit is still cut off from them and they are only receiving secondary energies or using the momentum of God that has been given to them as their original portion. When that portion is through, when they have squandered and misqualified it, they have no further access to the plane of Spirit.

In the parable, we see that there are two rewards given to those who fulfill the law of self-transcendence. First, they are made a ruler in the Matter plane. "I am the Guru in the plane of Spirit," says the lord in the parable. "Now you may represent me in the plane of Matter because you have proven that when I give you an increment of light, you will justly and lawfully multiply it to the glory of God and to the service of man." So they are made rulers "over many things." Having that rulership, they have that heirship of a son or daughter and they have the right to rule over things, people, and circumstances.

This is the establishment of hierarchy by initiation, not by the "favorite son" concept. There were no favorites in the parable. All three individuals had equal opportunity. The law was impartial and impersonal, except that it gave each one "according to his several ability," which was the fulfillment of the law itself.

So the first reward is you will be a ruler in the plane of Matter over those who have not yet passed this initiation. The second reward is that I am according you entrance into the plane of Spirit, entrance into the joy of the lord, entrance into my God consciousness.

The Carnal Mind and the Guru

If God had set up rules to the game by saying, "If you do these fifty things, then you will be able to have your ascension, or go to heaven," there are all kinds of self-seeking and selfish people in the world—and such people are flooding the churches today because they fear their own judgment—who would do every one of those fifty things to the letter, but their subconscious would still be filled with hatred and viciousness and desire for the manipulation of the light of the teacher.

I have seen such individuals. I have seen individuals meticulously follow this or that direction, and I have seen that grace is withheld because of impure motive, just as Cain's offering was not received because it was not acceptable in the sight of God. Cain's service, his sacred labor, was not acceptable because his motive was impure. His offering was given in a spirit of vain competition and jealousy of his brother Abel.[12]

God knows the carnal mind. He not only sets up his Law and his covenants. He also sets up that flame of grace and the guru-chela relationship because he knows that it is the hardest thing for the carnal mind of the individual disciple to submit to the Christ mind of his teacher.

As long as the disciple is in the carnal mind, he cannot perceive the Christ mind in his teacher. Looking through his own eyes, looking through his own carnal mind, he will accuse the teacher of being that carnally minded one. And so the Bible says that no man can confess that Jesus is Lord except by the Holy Ghost.[13] The Holy Ghost is the grace of God enabling you to transcend your carnal mind even before you have the

fullness of your Christ consciousness. Unless you have the Holy
Spirit that enables you to perceive the living Christ in the Guru
when he is rebuking you, cleaving asunder the Real from the
unreal, the carnal mind within will accuse the master himself of
being Satan and of being Antichrist.

Aside from his Law, God has given us the glorious person
of the Lord Jesus Christ so that we may not simply follow a
principle and say, "I have arrived." We have to come under the
tutelage of a person who has already attained to that principle.

This is the ancient teaching of the Hindus that has come
down from Lemuria, down from the great temples of the
Mother flame. Without that sacred, intimate relationship with
the Guru, even if we fulfill the requirements of the Law, we
may not be purged of our spiritual pride, our ego, our rebellion, our sensuality, our little self-deceptions, and all of those
things that have no place in the kingdom of heaven. Those are
the things that Shiva* destroys. And he always comes as a
person.

---

* The Hindu Trinity of Brahma, Vishnu, and Shiva is parallel to the Western
Trinity of Father, Son, and Holy Spirit. The three form the triad for the creation,
preservation, and destruction of the universe. Shiva, the Destroyer (also known as
the Restorer), is the fearsome one who drives away sin, disease, and demons of
delusion.

Rebellion against God

Then he which had received the one talent came and said, Lord, I knew thee that thou art an hard man, reaping where thou hast not sown, and gathering where thou hast not strawed: And I was afraid and went and hid thy talent in the earth: lo, there thou hast that is thine.

What happens to the third chela? He returns with the one talent that he had received. The state of consciousness of this chela is the perversion of the energy of Father, Son, and Holy Spirit. He immediately enters into criticism, condemnation, and judgment of the Guru: "Lord, I knew thee that thou art an hard man, reaping where thou hast not sown, and gathering where thou hast not strawed."*

He is judging his Guru, and he is demonstrating his total ignorance of the law of self-transcendence and the law of multiplication, which is the requirement for the sustainment of life. His false perception of the Guru, who multiplies consciousness and receives the reward of that multiplication, has resulted in the chela's unrighteous judgment.

He sees the Guru with all this abundance, all this light—wealth both in Spirit and Matter—and he says, "Who do you think you are? You haven't earned that. We have to sweat by the work of our hands and by our karma, and how can you be living there with all that light and abundance? You owe me that light; you owe me your abundance." That is the thinking

---

* I.e., where you have not sown any seed

of one who is carnally minded, who will not submit to the one who has become the Christ.

This unrighteous judgment of the Guru is, in fact, the judgment of the Father and of his Law. It is the perversion of the power and authority of the hierarch and of the order of hierarchy. This chela is challenging the Guru's right to be Guru. He is challenging the right of the Guru to be the Father principle, the Lawgiver incarnate, to set up the law of his chelaship, its covenant, its requirements—which are specifically for this chela: "Take this one talent, multiply it, and bring it back to me."

This chela is saying, "Why should I take this substance you're giving me, go out and work hard, and then bring back to you what I've earned by *my* labor? You don't have any right to the increase on this one talent."

The denial of that right of the Guru to occupy the position of the Father actually denies Almighty God the option of dwelling in the temple of the chosen one. The chosen one is not a favorite son. The chosen one is simply the one who has chosen to be God.

What this chela is saying is, "God, you don't have any right to live in the temple of a mere finite being, a mere mortal, a mere man who is appearing before me and exacting requirements of the law." That is the word of the fallen ones, who have entered the Matter plane and said, "God, you do not have any right whatsoever to live within your children, and if you try to live within your children and you try to set up an order of hierarchy in the governments and the economies of the nations, I will murder and destroy you."

The ignorance of this chela always begins with his ignoring of the Law. It's the perversion of the Word incarnate, the supreme reason or Logos, which is the foundation of all lesser laws, such as that of the law of transcendence or the law of the multiplication of the loaves and the fishes.

So first he denies the Guru as Father, and then he ignores the wisdom or the teaching of the Son. This then manifests as that fear that is the denial of the perfect love of the Holy Spirit. He acknowledges this fear: "And I was afraid and went and hid thy talent in the earth: lo, there thou hast that is thine." He is in a state of fear because he has alienated himself from the Law of the Father and from the teaching of the Son.

Whereas perfect love of the Holy Ghost, of the Father, and of the Son through the Guru would have resulted in the chela's manifest ability to multiply his substance, the absence of this perfect love is demonstrated in his chastisement of the Guru with a rebuke filled with sarcasm and mockery. This very chastisement of the Guru deprives him of the light of the Trinity, which is the essential element in the alchemy of the multiplication of talents. All things are wrought in this Matter plane in the name of the Father and of the Son and of the Holy Ghost. When we ignore this teaching of Jesus Christ, whether in the spirit or the letter of the law, we deprive ourselves of the abundant life.

Those who are like this servant, who have denied the Trinity, have therefore evolved other systems and other methods in order to circumvent the Trinity. In fact, it is they themselves who reap where they have not sown and gather where they have not strawed, doing the very things of which they have accused those who have gone before them, obediently, wisely, and lovingly on the path of initiation.

Only the Guru can deal with this rebellion. This same rebellion is in the fallen ones throughout the planetary body today, who have set themselves up as heads of state, heads of nations, heads of the banking systems and the economies.

Who challenges them? Who will come along and rebuke them and strip them of the misqualified energies that they have taken from the children of God and will seize from them their power?

No one dares challenge them because no one has understood that there are only two people who can challenge a fallen one who is in this state of rebellion. These two people are the Guru himself, the ascended master, or his embodied chela when

that chela is acting in the name of the Guru, in the name of the
I AM THAT I AM, in the name of the Lord Jesus Christ, and
when that chela is in perfect alignment with his Guru.

A chela may think he is a chela, but if he has compromised
the Father through the condemnation of his Guru and the
ignorance of his law, if he has compromised the Son by the
failure to implement his light and teaching, if he is trembling in
fear and doubt and anxiety and does not have the perfect love
of the Holy Ghost, then he is no chela. He may go up to someone in power in this world and challenge him, but the challenge
will fall to the ground and the one in power will simply laugh,
because the fallen ones will laugh at you in derision until you
demonstrate power.

Power is the only thing that talks. People say money talks.
Money is an interpretation of power. It is the power of the
ascended masters, it is the power of the Word incarnate in their
chelas that is the only force able to rebuke this energy.

The Rebuke

Thou wicked and slothful servant, thou knewest that I reap where I sowed not, and gather where I have not strawed: Thou oughtest therefore to have put my money to the exchangers, and then at my coming I should have received mine own with usury.

First of all, the Guru rebukes this servant for his wickedness and his slothfulness. This is the turning upon the servant of the condemnation that he has heaped upon the head of the Guru. He denounces the chela as a wicked and slothful servant. This is not criticism. It is not condemnation. It is not human judgment. It is the fire of the Holy Spirit that separates the Real from the unreal.

The most cherished word you will ever receive from the Guru is the chastisement that separates light and darkness—not by condemnation but by the sacred fire. Naming those conditions of consciousness is like naming the demons.* They are forced to come out. The individual is forced to choose whether he will remain in the service of those conditions or whether he will now be in the service of the living Christ.

It is a very sacred moment when the Guru loves you enough to tell you that you are a slothful and wicked servant and then gives you the teaching, which is the next action of the Guru in the parable. First, he defines the chela's state of

---

* Mark 5:9 and Luke 8:30 record that when Jesus sought to cast "unclean spirits" out of a man, he first asked, "What is thy name?" The name is the key to the vibratory pattern of a demon, also known as an entity.

Adam and Eve Expelled from Eden.
Through disobedience to the laws of the Mystery School, Adam and Eve rejected the Guru, so the world must become their teacher.

consciousness. Next, he corrects his ignorance of the law by giving him the teaching: "You should have gone and put my money to the exchangers, and I should have received mine own with interest."

The Guru explains to the chela that it is the law of the cosmos that the Guru who has attained the fullness of Alpha and Omega does not have to go through the normal channels of work, which became the law of karma after the expulsion of Adam and Eve from the Garden of Eden.

The Bible records that God said to the woman, "I will greatly multiply thy sorrow and thy conception; in sorrow thou shalt bring forth children; and thy desire shall be to thy husband, and he shall rule over thee."[14] And God said to Adam, "In the sweat of thy face shalt thou eat bread, till thou return unto the ground; for out of it wast thou taken: for dust thou art, and unto dust shalt thou return."[15] And Adam went forth to till the ground from whence he was taken. That was the karma for disobedience to the Guru.

Now what does the chela say who rebels against his karma? "If you have placed this karma upon me that I have to toil by the sweat of my brow, I say to you that you must do the same. You must work and toil and sweat with me." In other words, "You have to come down to my level, because we all have to be equal." He accuses the Guru of sowing where he has not strawed, because the chela is not able to perceive the investment.

God is the greatest investor of the cosmos. He perpetually invests his Spirit into his servant sons, from the great solar hierarchies, to the Elohim, all the way to the elementals. And by the grace of his Holy Ghost and by the wisdom of the Law, the multiplication of energy daily returns to God vast increments of energy, consciousness, and being. That is the right of the God-free being. It is the law of God. It is the law of the One who has become God.

It is your prerogative as you attain to higher consciousness to use the higher Law of Alpha and Omega to manifest by the alchemy of the Holy Spirit the virtue, supply, light, energy, and consciousness that are necessary to your individual evolution. The Guru has become the law of First Cause incarnate. He no longer has any need of the things of this world. Therefore, the multiplication of his abundance comes through the extension of his consciousness through his chelas.

How does Morya, the Guru, multiply himself? You become Morya. There is a net gain to the universe of the will of God as you become El Morya, and that accrues to his bank account, as it lawfully should, because he is the original investor. He has given to you the momentum of his will of God. If you have gained by it, you owe him who has provided the capital for you to multiply. Whenever we attain under any guru, he thereby gains higher attainment. He moves on in initiation. It's the lawful giving of a portion of the self to the one who has made the expansion possible.

We bring the fruit of our sacred labor to the feet of the Guru gladly. This fruit of higher consciousness is then in turn multiplied by the Guru and given back to the chelas, who use it once again to multiply and increase the great spheres of their own causal bodies.

The Guru, who abides in the white-fire core of Alpha and Omega, is subject to laws of the Spirit, whereas the chelas in the multiplication of God consciousness are subject to the laws of Matter, time and space, and their own individual karma and dharma. The Guru's wise counsel to this chela, therefore, is that if he himself was not willing or able to multiply his talent, the least he could have done would have been to return to the Guru his talent with the normal interest due from the exchangers. "And then at my coming I should have received mine own with usury"—the interest which always returns on the investment of Spirit in Matter.

God has an investment in the Matter cosmos. He expects a return, and it is the increase of light that comes from your personal crystallization of the God flame.

The Fiery Trial

Take therefore the talent from him, and give it unto him which hath ten talents. For unto every one that hath shall be given, and he shall have abundance: but from him that hath not shall be taken away even that which he hath.

Because the third servant has obeyed neither the laws of Spirit nor the laws of Matter, neither the laws of the guru-chela relationship nor the laws of his own karma, the judgment is placed upon him that the talent he has been given should be taken from him and given to the one who has assiduously multiplied the talent according to the laws of both Spirit and Matter. And here is the statement of the law: "For unto every one that hath shall be given, and he shall have abundance; but from him that hath not shall be taken away even that which he hath."

That is a universal law of the Christ, and at certain periods of the evolution of humanity, that law is placed like an electrode of cosmic consciousness within the earth body.* As that law begins to outwork itself, you will begin to see that those who work righteousness increase in righteousness, and those who work in unrighteousness decrease because the energy is taken from them.

The stripping from this chela of that which he has not

---

* Sanat Kumara reintroduced this very law and its action upon the planetary body in a dictation given March 29, 1964, published in *Pearls of Wisdom*, vol. 42, no. 38, September 19, 1999.

rightfully achieved by his own inner flame is the action of the fiery trial of the Holy Ghost, which must come to each of us. It's the initiation which Jesus passed through, the tenth of the fourteen stations of the cross, which is "Jesus is stripped of his garments." That initiation is upon you and me right now in the action of the Lord's judgment.

According to the law, this initiation states that all that we have not gained by the inner attainment of our own God consciousness must be taken from us in the hour of the coming of the fiery trial. This is the love of God. It's the most intense, fiery love of God, that his sons and daughters learn the laws of creation and of becoming a co-creator with him by the correct use of free will.[16]

God has no attachment to those things with which individuals in this world surround themselves unlawfully, dishonestly, outside of the path of initiation, outside of the Father, the Son, and the Holy Spirit. Therefore in the fiery trial, the individual must surrender all that he has taken from life without passing energy through the Trinity, without the guru-chela relationship.

The chela stands naked before his Guru, as he will stand in the judgment naked before his Creator, stripped of all but that which he has increased through obedience to the law of self-transcendence, through illumination of the law of multiplication based on the utter love of the chela for the Guru, the disciple for Jesus Christ, and yes, the employee for the employer. The chela would learn nothing from being allowed to keep the one talent without increase. But he will learn a great deal by being stripped of that talent.

The one who has multiplied his talents can now be trusted to receive that talent and more. The light he has gained, he has multiplied. He will be given more light because he has shown himself to be a just steward of the energies of God, a profitable servant, a wise investor.

Karma and the Law

And cast ye the unprofitable servant into outer
darkness: there shall be weeping and gnashing of teeth.

Finally there comes another pronouncement upon the chela. He has been rebuked. He has been told what he should have known as the true teachings of the Christ and what he should have done with his money. He has had his talent stripped from him. These are the three actions of the Trinity.

Now we come to the action of the fourth ray, the white ray of discipline, the white ray of the Mother, the white ray of the ascension. The chela is cast outside of the circle of the guru-chela relationship. He will no longer have contact with the person of God.

This is the reenactment of the drama of the putting forth of Adam and Eve from the Garden of Eden because of their disobedience. Jesus stands on that very law and that very principle. Thus the chela must now learn to deal with his own karma outside of the circle of this intimate relationship of Christ and his disciples. The world will be his guru.

The world will consist of planetary karma, to which he has contributed by his offense against the Deity in many incarnations and by his personal karma. The world, as personal and planetary karma, will be his teacher. He will learn by the Law itself. The impersonal law will be his teacher, because he has denied the personal law in the person of God's representative.

The impersonal law is much more harsh than the personal law. We saw the action of the impersonal law throughout the period of the prophets and the patriarchs in the Old Testament: instant karma, instant descent of that law. It's shocking to think of the things that happen in the Old Testament: sudden death, sudden destruction, absolute judgment coming through the hand of the prophets. Take Lot's wife, for instance. She is given one direction: Don't look back when you leave Sodom. She turns her head and looks back and she becomes a pillar of salt.[17] That is the law of impersonal karma descending instantaneously without the intermediary of the individual Christ.

Throughout that dispensation, from the departure from the Garden of Eden to the coming of the Lord Jesus Christ, people were under the impersonal law because they had denied the personal Guru, the Cosmic Christ, Lord Maitreya. The LORD God sent his only-begotten Son into the world, the Lord Christ who incarnated in Jesus. Once again grace transcends the Law, and if we are disobedient, we are rebuked, chastised, disciplined, and God gives us another chance.

The path of initiation and the path of the ascension at least has a chance in our lives when we have the person of the ascended masters, the person of the Guru. The weeping and gnashing of teeth is the condition of dealing directly with one's own returning karma without the intercession of the Trinity, without the presence of the Guru, who helps the chela to carry the cross of personal and planetary karma until he is able.

The Guru carries the cross of the chela's karma so that the chela can go out and perform a sacred labor to balance that karma. The chela cannot carry the cross and balance his karma simultaneously. That has been proven over hundreds of thousands of years. The people of this planetary body have so much karma that they need the periodic incarnation of the avatars so that the karma can be upon the back of the Son of God, so that the chela can say, "Now I can go out and perform that service and balance that karma so that I may attain my victory."

This is a tremendous opportunity. We think we hold world karma, but we hold only a portion of it. The karma which we balance daily by the violet flame is but a token of that which we have done against God. It's all that the law requires us to balance in that day, because dealing with that token demonstrates obedience to the Law and a willingness to meet our own personal human consciousness in the process.

None of us really knows how much karma we would have to balance if suddenly everything we had ever misqualified for the last million years were placed upon us. We could not bear it. To receive that karma all at once would be instant death.

There is no relationship that is legitimate other than the guru-chela relationship. It may seem impractical, but it is not. All of the nations of the earth, all of the economies, all of the governments must come under this relationship, because none of those individuals who purport to represent the people could in any way, shape, or form carry the cross of the people, carry their karma, or even their own karma.

Only those servant sons who have balanced a certain portion of their karma and who are one with those who have balanced *all* of their karma, the ascended masters, can stand in the world today and challenge evil incarnate in the fallen ones.

Respect for Hierarchy

This parable of beloved Jesus establishes the necessity for a free-market economy in order for the individual to pass his initiations on the path of individual Christhood. It establishes equal opportunity according to each one's individual talents. It establishes a system of rewards according to one's sacred labor. It illustrates that those rewards are not forthcoming unless the very foundation of the sacred labor be the Trinity and the acknowledgment of the Father, the Son, and the Holy Ghost as indwelling within the soul, as indwelling within the individual who is one's immediate superior, one's hierarch, one's guru, one's teacher, parent, administrator, or whoever is over one in life.

The acknowledgment of a person in authority is never based upon the outer manifestation. This is unrighteous judgment. Our real guru is our karma, and the one who may be over us presently may be the very embodiment of that karma and of those conditions within our own consciousness that we must come to grips with.

We may cry out and say, "That person is dishonest, that person is unjust, that person is hateful. I will not allow that person to be my superior." But that is not the point. In that person is God the Father, the Son, and the Holy Spirit, who is the real Guru. The real person we are serving is God.

The reason we are seeing an imperfect guru is because that person is the reflection of our own karma. Our karma must be our teacher. So we must come under someone who is a tyrant or perhaps someone who is phlegmatic and indecisive—and we get exasperated because they can never make a decision. And we know exactly what they should be doing and we would like to tell them, but we are not in a position to do so. That's because we have been a tyrant or indecisive in a previous life.

The real person we are serving is Jesus Christ within that temple. "Inasmuch as you have done it unto the least of these my brethren, ye have done it to me."[18] So if Jesus places "the least of these my brethren" over you, then serve God within him until you so serve and so love that God that you pass all the tests that person is capable of giving you and you transmute the karma that person presents as a reflection of your own. When there has been harmony and the resolution of the causes behind the need for that relationship, you will be promoted to a higher grade and you will get the next guru, and you will think, "Why, it's so wonderful I now have this marvelous teacher after all of these other terrible teachers I've had."

The fact is that you have balanced your karma, so now you are seeing the image of your own Christ Self more clearly, standing before you in the person of the one who is now giving you your initiations.

A Free-Market Economy

When the free-market economy is based on the law of the abundant life and the Golden Rule, "Do unto others as you would have them do unto you," when the Golden Rule is enshrined as the rule of the Christ in every heart, there need never be imposed from without by government any restraints whatsoever. You do not have to restrain a free-market economy or a free-enterprise system except to control the evil within individuals, except to control the carnal mind.

We have restraints imposed by our government, by Federal Reserve regulations. We would not need these if we were a nation that had accepted the inheritance of the guru-chela relationship under Jesus Christ and Saint Germain. We would have the inner restraint imposed on us from within, by our own Christ Self, because the individual has submitted his will to the will of God for the greater good of the community. This is the inner law of the Trinity functioning in its regulatory aspect.

We do not need all kinds of regulatory agencies to regulate our souls and our private lives and taxing and regulating the flow of our money. All of that regulation is not needed except for the presence of those who are called "the spoilers." They are the ones who come to spoil the guru-chela relationship. They tear it down and they say, "We will have the light-energy-consciousness of the Guru *without* the Guru. We will take the light, we will manipulate, and we will abuse and misuse the system."

The regulatory aspect is the power of God within you, his Law written in your inward parts,[19] his energy, his light.

Wisdom is his intelligence, which enables us to make wise investments for sound returns for business, for our family, for our community. All of our endeavors come about on the basis of wise investment of energy, time, and space. And finally, love is the very energy itself invested for the good of the people.

But what do you find in the abuses of the system of Capitalism today? You find the commercialization of drugs, alcohol, and tobacco. All of these are anti-love. They would be eliminated from the true economy simply by the Golden Rule. The businesses of the fallen ones and their abuse of the light of the children of God would be eliminated automatically if sons and daughters of God within this nation would hold to the line of the guru-chela relationship.

When the standards of the Trinity are compromised, the system must ultimately collapse. When the individual fails to humble himself before the inner light of God, his power, before the inner consciousness, the Son, and before the inner energy, the Holy Spirit, the individual too collapses. And though there are empires built and billions of dollars made within these industries, the individuals who have created them come to naught. Their inner systems collapse, they degenerate, they die of diseases or of sudden deaths or accidents. They are judged, for they have squandered their light and their souls. They are cast into outer darkness or they pass through the second death.[20]

El Morya has said that we should not be concerned when we see our neighbors or other people getting away with breaking the laws of God and accumulating vast amounts of wealth and seeming to be full of human happiness. He said that we count a single lifetime as a very short period in the epoch of man's evolution, and we do not always see the outcome of the Law. But we know the Law is in action and the Law is working. And there has never been a civilization that could survive without being founded upon the Trinity, because the Trinity is actually the white-fire core nucleus of the substance of Matter itself. Matter itself must collapse when the Trinity is ignored.

The law of self-transcendence and the law of multiplication, as they are illustrated in the parable of the talents, show that Jesus Christ himself ordained profit and the profit motive. These were not for competition between individuals, but a means whereby the individual could have a constant measure of his own progress on the ladder of life. This ladder of initiation is verily Jacob's ladder[21] whereby the soul ascends from Matter to Spirit according to his self-mastery in the Law.

Competition with oneself results in balance and equilibrium within a free-market economy, because it allows individuals to compare their own achievements and quality of excellence to those of others within their various fields of endeavor. This provides a standard for quality and price control in the manufacture of goods and in the rendering of service.

The Law of the Tithe

The net gain of the multiplication of talents always belongs to God or to the God-man, the Guru. Such a one was Melchizedek, "king of Salem, which is king of peace; without father, without mother, without descent, having neither beginning of days, nor end of life; but made like unto the Son of God."[22]

Melchizedek is the priest, and to him Abraham gave a tenth of the spoils. He gave a tenth of his increase. On earth that is what God requires. God didn't say to give it to just any organization or any church. He said it belongs to Melchizedek, who is God incarnate. The tenth belongs where you have the incarnation of the Word, where you have a church or a charity whose people are working together for the good of humanity—not based on a scientific humanism but based on the Father, the Son, and the Holy Spirit—who acknowledge their discipleship under Jesus Christ or under Gautama Buddha or under Shiva.

The foundation of the Trinity must be where you tithe, because you are tithing to God. You are returning the energy you have received to the fiery core. So you don't just tithe anywhere. You can't just give your tithe to cancer research and say that is your just tithe.

The tithe belongs to Melchizedek. It belongs to the one that God has sent for the multiplication of his Being. And in the absence of people perceiving that God incarnate, when they contribute to their churches that are founded upon Christ even though there may be a dispute or a difference of doctrine or

Abraham and Melchizedek.
Genesis 14 describes how
Abraham met Melchizedek,
king of Salem, who served
him bread and wine.
Abraham gave Melchizedek a
tenth of all the spoils of the
battle he had just won.

dogma, the energy is still taken as the token that is given to God as long as it is being used lawfully.

When a church appropriates vast sums of money for Communist guerrillas in Africa,[23] that is no longer a lawful use of the tithe, and those who are tithing to that church must realize that they are no longer giving their funds to a representative of the priest after the Order of Melchizedek. So you must be mindful where you give your tithe, because for your energy to multiply you must give it to the ascended masters or their representatives who are carefully carrying out the will of God.

The reason that we give the tenth back to God is because it is then multiplied by ten and returned to us. We give 10 percent to God. We receive 100 percent in return—another increment, another five talents or two talents or one talent with which we can go out and increase our God consciousness. You cannot experience the fullness of the abundant life if you do not respect this law.

When as much as 70 percent of people's earnings goes for taxation, as it does in Socialist countries, how can individuals possibly tithe and give their lawful amount to God? This is precisely the point of the interference of the fallen ones in our government and our economy. Right and left, they are determined to deprive us of our proper association with the Godhead.

Morya said to me, "No matter how poor an individual is, he can still fulfill the law of the tithe. If all he has is a bowl of rice that is his daily food and in that bowl there are ten spoonfuls of rice, it will not make or break him to give one spoonful back to God."

So whether we happen to be the poorest or the wealthiest of people, there is always something that we have of which a tenth may be tithed. And if it is not tithed, there is no basis for its multiplication.

The Spiritual Role of America

America is a nation whose people and government are intended to be in the state of chelaship. Those nations who have and to whom is given more because they have correctly exercised the law of the abundant life, move into the position of guru relative to the other nations of the earth. A nation such as America, which has the abundance of God because its individual members have correctly applied the teachings of Jesus Christ, must always remember not to abuse its office in hierarchy. If it does, it may also be subject to the judgment.

We are under that judgment today. It is not lawful for America to give vast sums of money to nations who squander that money, without America exacting the multiplication of the talent. We have seen many cases where the leaders of nations who have been the recipients of gifts from America have abused and squandered that money while the poor have gone without the food, medical aid, and clothing for which the supply was designated.[24] In contrast to this, representatives of our country have gone into underdeveloped countries and taught the people to become independent and self-reliant.[25] That is the real teaching of the Guru.

There comes a time then when individuals who enter into condemnation of America through the ignorance of the law and who by their own state of fear and doubt are not multiplying in love the light of the Holy Spirit, must be put outside of the circle of oneness. It is not lawful for America to give financial aid to Communist nations controlled by fallen ones who are engaged in the slaughter of the holy innocents, who are placing Christians, Jews, and others in concentration camps, subjecting them to torture because of their faith or their desire to be free. Likewise it is not lawful for us to give technology, wheat, science, and all of the gifts of the abundant life to such nations. When America is disobedient to that law, we are violating our own guru-chela relationship and we will be cut off from the light of the Guru because we have forgotten that the light and energy of our resources are not ours.

Our resources are a gift on loan, and we are expected to multiply the talent according to the covenant set by the Guru, which says, "This is the light and the abundance of the Mother. It may only be used for the children of the Mother to increase their Christ consciousness." This essence of the Christ consciousness was not given to America to be given away to the fallen ones. This is a violation of a sacred trust, and America is thereby being cut off from her lawful relationship with the ascended masters. The only reason that she continues to hold any relationship whatsoever is because the few chelas of the ascended masters are abiding by the Law and keeping the flame and holding the balance.

The principle is the same as when Lot asked God to spare the city if ten righteous people could be found in Sodom.[26] They were not found, and the city was destroyed. Today there are the ten righteous (or the percentage required in the United States of America), and that alone is what holds this nation, this economy, this government together, and not all of the solutions of the power elite.

Neither those who are in power nor all of their solutions can hold this nation together. It is held together by the trust of the people. That trust is in the figure-eight flow between the disciple and the Christ. And there are many beautiful people today in Christian churches who are disciples of Christ to the very best of their ability, in spite of doctrine and dogma, and they too are holding the balance for America.

The Challenge

We must not believe the lie of the Serpent that Socialist or Communist systems or the manipulation of Capitalist systems will be the solution to the problems of this nation or any nation. The Law is not so, and we must live by the laws of God.

It is not lawful for lightbearers to be giving to the fallen ones, who have refused to come under the disciplines of the hierarchy of the Great White Brotherhood, any aspect of our money or technology, which they in turn use to kill and destroy the children of the light so that they may take by force the power that they have not been willing to earn by lawful means.

It is also not lawful for the lightbearers within this nation to tolerate the abuses of the free-market system, which pave the way for the destruction of the path of initiation through the economy and thereby open the way for an ungodly Socialism and an atheistic Communism. As lightbearers, we must challenge the abuses of the free-market and the free-enterprise system in America. We personally must challenge that which is a violation of our personal relationship to our personal Guru. It is not enough to know that it is wrong. We will compromise our own relationship to God if we stand by and do nothing.

The abuses of the free-enterprise system in America today by the fallen ones—the hoarding of goods, the elimination of competition, the manipulation of our supply and our currency —all of this is making America vulnerable to becoming a welfare state, and the welfare state is no part of the guru-chela relationship. If it had been, Jesus' parable would have been different.

The Federal Reserve Act of 1913 gave the banking community control of the nation's money in violation of Article I, Section 8, of the Constitution. The Fed can expand or contract the supply of money and credit, unilaterally creating economic policy. It was irresponsible manipulation of the money supply that brought about the inflation of the 1920s, the crash of 1929, and the Great Depression, and so the presumed requirement for a Roosevelt New Deal, which greatly expanded and centralized government control and manipulation of the economy.

The Guru would have patted the back of the one who brought back one talent and said, "You're absolutely right. I haven't earned it. I don't have any right to it. You can have it and you can have my Christ consciousness and you can be made a ruler over my children." All of that would have been in the parable. It is not there precisely because that would not have been lawful.

People have a tremendous fear to challenge the fallen ones, and this is what we are up against today. And so the Holy Spirit has come to destroy the abuses of the free-market economy, such as creating monopolies, restraining free trade, regulating prices and wages, seizing control of vital commodities such as food, manipulating the flow of energy sources such as oil, electricity, and coal, and the creation and management of inflation for selfish ends.

The control and coining of money has been taken from the hands of the people, from Congress, and placed in the hands of a self-governing power elite posing as the enlightened ones. Gold has been removed from playing an active role in the economy. The ownership and control of land and the means of production is more and more centralized.

All of this is happening in the United States of America today, and it is the abuse of the guru-chela relationship. Once you destroy that relationship, you destroy the path of the ascension. Once you destroy the path of the ascension, there is no goal in life. And if you destroy the goal in life, you destroy hope. When the flame of hope goes out—the hope that an individual by his sacred labor may attain to excellence, may self-transcend himself—you have destroyed the person. He might as well be a robot or a humanoid.

This is what is happening to the people in Eastern Europe, in Russia, and in Communist China today. They are no longer people. They are a "kind of man," a *man-kind*, but they have been deprived of their joint heirship with Christ,[27] save for those few who are willing to suffer persecution unto the death to preserve their guru-chela relationship, who will die before they deny their Lord and Saviour Jesus Christ.[28]

These are the martyrs of the underground church of Russia, Hungary, Bulgaria, Czechoslovakia. They are living witnesses to the truth that there is nothing more important than the name of God, I AM THAT I AM. For it is by the name of God we are saved, the name of the one who has become God—the name of Jesus Christ, the name of Saint Germain, the name of the entire Spirit of the Great White Brotherhood.

We begin with that premise. We begin with the cosmic honor flame, which is the Trinity become the white light. So this is what we are about. We are here to preserve the integrity of the guru-chela relationship, and by preserving that integrity, we will preserve a nation under God and then many nations under God and then earth and all her evolutions—Home and free.

The Religious Philosophy
of Karl Marx

The Origins of Evil

When the original archdeceivers penetrated the state of bliss that we knew in our origin and began to deny the LORD God and the manifestation of the Son and of the Holy Ghost, this was the beginning of duality. This was the beginning of the necessity for time and space, for life and death, for relative good and evil.

That rebellion began with an archangel, who was therefore in the hierarchy of hosts of the LORD even above the sons and daughters of God. The angels and the archangels were created by the LORD God first in the order of creation because they were created to expand the desire body of God—God's desiring to be God, the ensoulment of his virtue, the ensoulment of his consciousness.

The ensoulment of God's power to create was transferred to the ones who were the very portion of Himself, the archangels and the angels. Their very name implies their office, which is to be the *angle* of God's consciousness. They are the many facets, the many jewels, the points of light, the angles of God's Being ensouled throughout a Spirit-Matter universe vibrating and quivering at the original point and flame of Alpha and Omega, without the dense spheres of being.

These angelic hosts felt their equality with God because they were indeed the very portion of that living fire, as God dipped into the sacred fire of his heart to create them—living spirit sparks whom he called seraphim, cherubim, angels, and orders of angels, who throughout a cosmos actually sustain the *antahkarana*, the geometry of a forcefield, the cradle of cosmos into which the Father-Mother God would place the only begotten Son, who is multiplied again and again in many servant sons and daughters. The Word became flesh in the descent of that Christ principle as the preserver of the Creation, and so the office of the sons and daughters of God is ordained, which is to preserve that which God has created in and of himself.

Because God placed within his sons and daughters the fullness of the Cosmic Christ, he drew all of the hosts of heaven together and he said, "This is my beloved son, hear ye him." However, when they assembled there was one among the archangels by the name of *Lucifer* (meaning "the bearer of light," the son of light, the son of the morning), who had great light and attainment. He said, "I will not bow down and worship the Son presence, the creation that thou hast made, for I am higher than that creation and I am at the level of God. I will not bend the knee and confess that the LORD God, the Lord Christ is incarnate in the sons and daughters of God, for I am superior to that creation."[29]

That one and his legions of angels became the original rebellious ones against the creation of God. Thus the denial of the Christ, which has become Antichrist throughout systems of worlds, was born in the mind of that one by spiritual pride and by ambition.

The descent of that Fallen One was the original Fall. That Fallen One placed himself above the LORD God, and taking with him his lieutenant Satan, Beelzebub, Belial, Serpent, the Adversary, and many others, they went forth. It is written that a third part of the angels of heaven were cast down,* falling through this original lie of the spiritual pride, the intellectualism of that one who dared to say, "I can run the universe better than God. I am superior to his sons and daughters, and

---

* "And there appeared another wonder in heaven; and behold a great red dragon, having seven heads and ten horns, and seven crowns upon his heads. And his tail drew the third part of the stars of heaven, and did cast them to the earth: and the dragon stood before the woman which was ready to be delivered, for to devour her child as soon as it was born" (Rev. 12:3–4).

Archangel Michael casting the fallen angels out of heaven. Gustave Doré, illustration for John Milton's *Paradise Lost.*

I refuse to acknowledge that the Christ is made flesh. I refuse to acknowledge that the Lord Jesus Christ is come in the flesh. I will refuse to acknowledge that every child of God has the potential to become the fullness of that Christ, because if I acknowledge that, then I would be acknowledging that the sons and daughters of God may exceed the attainment of the archangels and the Elohim. And I will not be removed from my superior position." This was the boasting of Lucifer.

> And there was war in heaven: Michael and his angels fought against the dragon; and the dragon fought and his angels, and prevailed not; neither was their place found any more in heaven. And the great dragon was cast out, that old serpent, called the Devil, and Satan, which deceiveth the whole world: he was cast out into the earth, and his angels were cast out with him.[30]

They were cast out of heaven into the earth, into the Matter planes, for the LORD God would no longer share the great sphere of unity of Alpha and Omega with those who would rebel against the Father as the Word and the authority and the Lawgiver, the Son as the incarnation of that Word, and the Holy Spirit as the glad-free gift of energy given to obedient sons and daughters to create and recreate and consummate the great love fire. Nor would the Father transfer to the Fallen One, to the rebellious ones, the manifestation of the Mother principle, the pure white fire that rises from the base chakra unto the crown, which is the ascension flame. Therefore these fallen ones were sealed off from the great and eternal light of God to which they had had access for aeons and aeons of time and space.

These fallen ones, who were rejected by the LORD God, in turn rejected his own servant sons and the incarnate Word. And because they no longer had access to the light of God, they had to devise schemes and plots and ploys to take from the children of light, to take from the sons and daughters of God, the energy to which they no longer had access.

Understanding the components of creation, understanding the nuclei of atoms and suns and galaxies, they understood the original principle of flow, the rhythm of Father, Son, and Holy Spirit—the movement of Brahma, Vishnu, and Shiva. To counteract the manifestation of the LORD God, they knew they would have to destroy and distort the rhythm of life itself—not simply a principle of Father, a principle of Son, a principle of Holy spirit, but the movement of energy of one superseding the other, of each building upon the other, and the self-transcendence and the perpetual building of energy, cycle upon cycle. They understood the rhythm of the beating of the heart, the inbreath and the outbreath, and they knew that the key to life and to creation was in the movement of cycles, and therefore, tampering with the cycles of being would be the key to the destruction of that creation.

Their revenge and their resentment and their vilification was an obsession of hatred of the LORD God, who had now denied them access to his sacred fire and to the fount of living flame. Their all-consuming revenge became a determination to sever the soul from its contact with the Trinity within the heart, to deny that Trinity, and to make the children of God forget that there ever was any Trinity within the heart, to forget that they could be the fullness of the Word incarnate, that they could be that full potential of being.

The seeds of the wicked and of the Fallen One have been sown in and out through the civilizations of Lemuria and Atlantis, and to the present hour. They have woven their diabolical lie that man is separated from God, that God does not care, that God does not hear, that God does not run his universe well enough. On this basis they have devised systems that would be a substitute for God's own mechanism for running his universe, which is the flow of the Trinity nourished and watered and fed by the fountain of the Mother light. The seeds of Antichrist have been sown East and West.

The original lie and every ramification of that lie must be destroyed. Every corollary principle as it has affected first the tie of the soul to the living God, which is religion,* and every false doctrine and dogma voiced by every false prophet and false Christ for thousands and thousands of years, even long before the era of Jesus Christ, must be destroyed. The earthen vessels must be broken, and the light of God must be poured into the true vessel, the chalice of being, the Holy Grail that is the sons and daughters of God.

Having now established a true relationship of the soul unto the living God and unto the Mother and the Trinity, now Shiva comes to break the earthen vessels of the false doctrine and the false dogma of the fallen ones as these have affected the governing of the flow of energy between the soul and God. That government ought to be upon the shoulders of the individual Christ Self, but it has been transferred by the diabolical lies of the fallen ones to the wicked, to the incarnate fallen angels. This must be stopped, and this rule of the fallen angels must be broken.

---

* The word *religion* comes from the Latin *religio*, from *religare*, meaning to "bind" or "tie back." The true purpose of religion is to bind the soul to God.

The fundamental lie of Satan has invaded our understanding of self-government, of the God-control of energy within us, and then of the government of the family, of the community, of the nation, and of the community of nations. That lie has been an earthen vessel into which the fallen ones have attempted to pour the precious light of God, the blood of the saints, the Body and the Blood of the Lord Jesus Christ. They have usurped the Eucharist, and they have evolved their false doctrine and dogma. They are the wolves in sheep's clothing.

And so comes Lord Shiva. He comes as the Destroyer. He enters. He performs his cosmic dance. He breaks the earthen vessel. He seizes once again the light of the saints that has been usurped by the fallen ones, and he pours it into that God-government that is proclaimed by the Lord Jesus Christ. We see that the government is now, can be, and forevermore shall be upon the shoulders of the individual Christ Self through Jesus Christ, through Saint Germain, and through all of the ascended masters who have become one with that flame.

The fallen ones have also invented their separatist doctrine in the flow of the abundant life, in the economies of the nations. They have seized the gold of the children of God, the supply, the wheat, the technology, the science—all of the abundance that flows from that fountain of living fire that is the Mother flame. So the Holy Ghost descends and reclaims that sacred fire that has been abused. For this abuse is the sin against the Holy Ghost,[31] that abomination of desolation standing in the holy place where it ought not.[32]

Therefore comes the Holy Ghost. Therefore comes the principle and the person of Lord Shiva. He breaks the earthen vessels. He seizes once again the light of the Woman and her seed. He returns that light to the sons and daughters of God, and he pours it once again into the chalice of the Holy Grail. Each individual child of God raises up his consciousness to receive that light, which therefore becomes the balance of the Trinity in religion, in government, in the economy.

The false doctrines of education whereby there is the

education of the outer mind to the neglect of the inner soul must also be broken by Lord Shiva. He comes to break the false doctrine and dogma that enters into our universities, our high schools, our elementary schools, our kindergarten and nursery schools—the false doctrine that the individual is not a soul, is not a spirit, alive and able to rise and soar, but it is a human species, a type of man, but not the fullness of God-man, not having the potential to realize that Godhood, that true individuality. This is the lie with which the youth and the children of this world have been programmed through the ages, denying the original genius of the Christ within the heart and the potential of that Christ to burst and flower and expand with a cosmic explosion of light that is truly the bursting of Cosmic Christ illumination.

Enter Lord Shiva to break these earthen vessels, to challenge the entire system of education in every nation upon earth, and to see that every little child from the hour of conception is honored as the incarnate Word, as the very presence of the living God, and to see that the soul is tutored to put on the garment of that cosmic consciousness from the very first breath. This is the coming of Shiva. This is the coming of the Holy Ghost. Shiva stands in the temple of the people, and he overthrows these diabolical systems programming our children and youth to believe the lie and therefore be damned by that lie in the karma that they make by the tantalizing schemes of the fallen ones.

Therefore the light of our youth is restored. It is returned to the chalice of the Holy Grail. And that light of the true education of the soul moving on the path of the Lord Christ is now returned to the heart of the Mother. By the hand of the Woman clothed with the Sun,[33] that energy of sacred fire is then returned to the children of God. They dance in the joy of springtime, and they are warmed by the blessed presence of the Mother. They receive the warm milk of the Word, and they understand that they are born of God, that they descend from his heart, that they ascend to his heart, and that there is indeed

no separation of the children of God from the original presence
of Alpha and Omega.

Now comes Lord Shiva to enter into the midst of the Mater
sphere, the Mater planes of being. And he breaks the earthen
vessels of the abuse of the science of the Woman, the science of
Omega, the science of the sons and daughters of God whereby
the crystallization of the God flame in Mater through science
and the abundant life is for the service of Christ, the king born
in each heart, the service of the soul on the path of initiation.
Every aspect of science should be in the service of the Lord
Christ East and West. And where science is in the service of
Antichrist, Shiva descends to break the earthen vessel, to
shatter the misuse of the Holy Ghost.

"'Vengeance is mine; I will repay,' saith the Lord."[34] "I will
reclaim the light and energy that the fallen ones have stolen,
and I am the victory, and I will have the victory." The LORD
God will seize that energy, and the proud spirits, the fallen ones
who think that that energy belongs to them, will fear and
tremble before the coming of the LORD God of hosts. For in the
moment when the LORD God of hosts allows the hand of the
LORD to descend in the Person of the Lord Jesus Christ, then
there is the shattering of the earthen vessels, and the fallen ones
stand naked before the LORD God. All energy of the Holy
Ghost that they have misused is instantaneously taken from
them, and they are as they were before they were born. And it
were better for them had they never been born than to have
abused the Holy Child of the Holy Christ within the sacred
temple of being.

Finally Lord Shiva comes in the culture of the Mother. He
comes in the very midst of art and music and drama and all of
the manifestations of the expression of the soul in life. He
shatters all manifestations that have been a misuse of the light,
of creativity, failing to glorify the LORD God but glorifying
instead the carnal mind and the rhythm of the fallen ones.

Shiva breaks those earthen vessels. He seizes those individuals who have abused the privilege of the flow of the Holy

Spirit. He breaks that momentum, and he shatters the disobedient creation. He frees the electrons and the molecules to return to the Great Central Sun of being.

He frees all life and energy and consciousness to sing the paeans of praise that the multitudes sing in the Book of Revelation as they sing unto the Lord a new song.[35] They sing the praise and the glory and the thanksgiving, the glory and the honor that are due unto the name of God, I AM THAT I AM.

The Garden of Eden

"God created man in his own image, in the image of God created he him"—Father, Son, and Holy Spirit. And God said:

> Be fruitful, and multiply, and replenish the earth, and subdue it: and have dominion over the fish of the sea, and over the fowl of the air, and over every living thing that moveth upon the earth....
>
> And God saw every thing that he had made, and, behold, it was very good....
>
> And the LORD God took the man, and put him into the garden of Eden to dress it and to keep it.
>
> And the LORD God commanded the man, saying, Of every tree of the garden thou mayest freely eat: but of the tree of the knowledge of good and evil, thou shalt not eat of it. For in the day that thou eatest thereof, thou shall surely die.[36]

Enter now the Serpent, the cohort of Satan. Serpent is the name of a fallen one who has misused the light of the Mother—the Kundalini fire, which is also often referred to as the serpentine force. The Archdeceiver of the woman is the one who has created the perversion of her own sacred fire, her own serpentine force, hence the name *Serpent*.

Serpent presents to the woman the illogical logic of the Fallen One, Lucifer, the counterpoint of the Logos, the mind of Christ:

Hath God said, Ye shall not eat of every tree of the garden?

And the woman said unto the serpent, We may eat of the fruit of the trees of the garden: but of the fruit of the tree which is in the midst of the garden, God hath said, Ye shall not eat of it, neither shall ye touch it, lest ye die.

And the serpent said unto the woman, Ye shall not surely die: for God doth know that in the day ye eat thereof, then your eyes shall be opened, and ye shall be as gods, knowing good and evil.

And when the woman saw that the tree was good for food, and that it was pleasant to the eyes, and a tree to be desired to make one wise,...[37]

The woman, saw that the manifestation of the Trinity in the tree of the knowledge of good and evil could be used for the adornment of the outer self. We find that Satan tempted Eve to partake of the energies of the Father, the Son, and the Holy Spirit—the power, the wisdom, and the love of God—and to use these to perpetuate a self-centered existence outside of God.

All subsequent desires of the human consciousness are a multiplication of these three desires. Each one of them is presented to Eve with the rationale of a good motive, that there will be some consequence of relative good as the result of disobedience to the LORD God.*

Through the critical eyes of the Serpent, the woman saw that the tree was "good for food." This was the temptation of the blue plume of power, the First Person of the Trinity, the Father. The Serpent showed the woman that the energy of the Father could be misqualified, or used as he put it, to gain all economic objectives in the world, to acquire wealth and all that was necessary to meet the demands of physical man. This was

---

* Lord Maitreya was the original initiator in that Mystery School, which was the Garden of Eden.

William Blake, *The Temptation and Fall of Eve* (Illustration for Milton's *Paradise Lost*) Misinterpretation of the account of Adam and Eve has tremendously distorted Christian beliefs about sin.

the justification for the misuse of the Father principle and the rejection of the Father's laws for the economic systems of the earth. This was the first temptation.

Second, through this eye of the Serpent, the woman saw that the fruit of the tree was "pleasant to the eyes." This is the pride of the eyes in the gratification of the senses and the emotions. It is the desire to fulfill the pleasures of these senses—the senses of the soul which God gave to us in the beginning so that we would become sensitive to the flow of his light, his Being, his love, and the Holy Spirit.

Now there could be the misuse of the light and energy of the Holy Spirit in the most diabolical perversions of life—all the way to the unspeakable perversions of sex itself, which have been occurring ever since that hour unto the present. This was the temptation to misuse the light of the Holy Ghost in all types of social interchange, in all the various exchanges of energies that occur in relationships of human attachment— even unto the perversion of the service of the priests and priestesses of the sacred fire in the temples of the Mother on Lemuria.

Finally, the woman saw that it was a tree to be "desired to make one wise." This is the temptation to replace the Christ mind with the carnal mind—to use the flame of the Son, the Second Person of the Trinity, in order to control the political movements of the world, to fulfill ambition, achievement, accomplishment, to gain power to manipulate others through that carnal mind. Eve was tempted to enter into the ways of the world.

As Jesus was tempted to fall down and worship Satan, who offered him "all the kingdoms of the world,"[38] the woman was tempted to fall down and worship the carnal mind as Serpent, who would give her dominion and power over all the kingdoms of the world—over all the planes of Matter and over all that she desired to have and to control in man.

When Eve saw what these misuses of the sacred fire could achieve, "She took of the fruit thereof and did eat and gave also unto her husband with her and he did eat."[39] This partaking of the flame of the Cosmic Christ for the elevation of the carnal mind is the original disobedience unto the LORD God. These three lies are fundamental to the destruction of every living soul.

Original Sin

Adam and Eve were twin flames given the opportunity to be initiated by the Cosmic Christ. We today are twin flames. You as an individual and your counterpart must encounter this Serpent as the carnal mind within you, who will attempt to make you abuse the flame of the Trinity, to use it for the aggrandizement of the self—both in the microcosm of your temple and in the Macrocosm of the world order.

These three desires—good for food, pleasant to the eyes, and a tree to be desired to make one wise—are at the foundation of human culture and human solutions to human problems. They permeate every endeavor and every field.

None of us can create except by the Trinity. When we misuse the energy of the Trinity because of one or two or three of our personal responses to these three lies, then we also have fallen for the lie of the Serpent. We are then removed from the mystery school. We are removed from the personal relationship to the Lord Christ, the incarnate Word, and we no longer have a path of initiation that is personal in association with the ascended masters, with the prophets, with the avatars of East and West. This has happened to most among mankind—even with the coming of Jesus Christ, who restored grace and restored the opportunity for the open door of the great Saviour, the great Guru, to once again allow us to pass through in obedience to his Word.

Original sin, then, is disobedience to God, and the corollaries of this disobedience remain veiled in the mists of maya. Mankind have not yet understood precisely what is this disobedience, believing that the Fall of man and woman in Eden had something to do with sex. If sex is the original sin, then we are all sinners.

That is the lie of the Fallen One. That is the lie that deters us from discovering this serpentine and very subtle logic by which it is not considered to be disobedience to the Lord Christ or a manifestation of the fallen consciousness to attempt to evolve human solutions to human problems according to these three temptations. We still think that by human reasoning and human logic we will arrive at perfect truth. This lie is the foundation for the overthrow of government, the economy, religion, science, and culture, that is being put upon the people today through World Communism.*

Now we move from the Serpent in the Garden, and we trace the lie of the Serpent specifically to the Big Lie invented by Satan—World Communism. Karl Marx's dialectical materialism, the very foundation of Communist doctrine, is founded on the subtle, Satanic lie first spoken to the woman in the Garden.

---

* At the time of this lecture, the movement to centralize power and control of the economies and the people of the world was embodied in World Communism. In the twenty-first century, the same goal is being pursued through the gradual imposition of socialist principles and ever greater control of the economy by national governments and the gradual surrender of their independence and sovereignty to transnational bodies. The strategy of military takeover has been replaced by incremental takeover. The goal of the fallen ones remains the same.

The Big Lie

The story of the Garden of Eden is not mythological, it is not a fairy tale, it is not fantasy. It is the story of two earnest people, whose names are given to us as Adam and Eve, twin flames having the opportunity just as we do today to pass their initiations.

Adam and Eve encounter a very suave and wise-appearing individual, very cultured, highly professional, very knowledgeable in the problems of the world and all of the culture of Lemuria and its colonies on the far-flung continents and all that was happening in the world at that time. He presents an alternative to the path of initiation and the path of the guru-chela relationship.

What he is really saying is that you can have both. You can have your relationship with the Cosmic Christ and the personal Christ, and you can also use the threefold flame* for these other human inventions. See what power the Father, the Son, and the Holy Ghost can give you. This Big Lie is only a hair removed from the original teachings of the Cosmic Christ.

So let us not think that we are looking into a distant past where the mist of Lemuria creates these mythological figures who are not like you and me. This record is so real it could have occurred five minutes ago to people just like us. And it *is* occurring right now, over and over again, in every nation, in every government, in every body of representatives of the

---

* The threefold flame is the "divine spark" within the heart of man and woman. It is also called the Christ flame or the liberty flame. The threefold flame is literally a spark of sacred fire from God's own heart. It is the soul's point of contact with the Supreme Source of all life.

people, among those who have seized their authority to represent the people and who do not have that authority from God because of their original rejection of the Lord Christ and his incarnation.

All government should be for the purpose of the unfoldment of that Christ presence, and therefore those who rule without that motive have no right to rule. All rulers should be the servants of the people—the servants of the Christ in the people. And those who are usurping the positions of the Trinity in government, the economy, science, education, and culture have no right to be there if they do not have this basic principle: "I am the servant of the Christ in the people, and Christ in me is that servant and is that one who governs, who performs the work."

Dialectic

Let us go right to the core of the matter. The Serpent engaged in the *dialectic*—discussion or debate in which opposing viewpoints initially advanced as contradictions (for instance, *thesis* versus *antithesis*) are resolved in a comprehensive outlook which embodies the substance of both. This resolution is called the *synthesis*.

In the Garden of Eden, the thesis is the teaching of the Cosmic Christ: exactly how one is to proceed with the appropriation of the sacred fire of the threefold flame, how one is intended to use the light of the Father, the Son, and the Holy Spirit for the expansion of consciousness, for taking dominion over the planes of Matter, for attainment and God-mastery, and for the conclusion of all of this, which is the ascension back to the fiery core of being.

The antithesis of Serpent says that you can use the Father, Son, and Holy Spirit to attain wealth, the gratification of the senses, and political power. By accepting some of the thesis, some of the antithesis, a synthesis is evolved. And that is precisely what you see today—a little bit of truth in religion, a little bit of lie. Mix them together and you get relative solutions to relative problems. We dwell in relative good and evil, a moving scale, and we have no sense that there is a measuring rod of the Law of God.

When we stand upon that Rock of Christ, that measuring rod becomes the fullness of God's power, wisdom, and love to resolve every human equation. But we live in a world of synthesis of good and evil, of light and darkness—of light that is a pure, crystal clear stream, and of that which has become a misqualification, a misinterpretation of that pure steam. It is like mixing oil and water. You can keep on mixing and stirring, and you will get a certain mixture, a certain emulsion. But as soon as you stop stirring, the oil and water separate.

The truth is that light and darkness can never mix. They may mix for a while, as Jesus described in his parable of the tares and the wheat.[40] They may combine for a while, they may grow side by side, they may be next to each other, and at some moments you cannot even tell them apart. But in the end when the God-harmony and the light of Alpha and Omega descend, when all is a cosmic stillness, light and darkness are clearly separate—*by vibration.*

"By their fruits ye shall know them."[41] By their fruits they separate. When you see the flower that comes out of the plant that is a rose, and the flower that comes out of the weed that is the thistle, you know what was the origin of each.

This synthesis of light and darkness is the basic premise that Marx used in the development of dialectical materialism. That philosophy was born in the mind of the Serpent in the Garden of Eden thousands of years ago right on Lemuria, right on the soil of the Motherland. The akashic records of the birth of that lie are there, and that seed of the Serpent has spawned until it has become the great red dragon of World Communism.

The only one who can challenge the lie is the Woman and her seed. By that I mean the Mother flame in you raised up in the full glory and adoration of the living God. It is the Mother in me, the Mother in you, the Mother in Omega and in all of the ascended masters, in all of the sons and daughters of God, that can and will overthrow this lie.

It is the feminine energy and the feminine principle in all of us that has fallen. Now we have the dispensation of the age of Aquarius and the coming of the Lord Shiva, who rescues the Woman and her seed.

Until this hour that lie has not been stayed. The lie has

been going on for thousands of years, and the children of God have believed this lie. They have believed it again and again in many different forms. Who has come to challenge that lie? The great avatars. They were the expression and the perfectionment of the Trinity, and they paved the way for the age when God Almighty would give to us once again the dispensation for the great mastery of the Mother flame.

Only when individual man and woman raise up once again the sacred fire of the Kundalini, the white light of the base of the spine, unto the crown, only then will they have the rod of Aaron, the rod of authority that will challenge these black magicians who have perpetuated the lie.* These black magicians have believed the lie, and they have led the people to believe in the lie.

Free people, God-fearing people all over the world, know that World Communism is destructive and diabolical, and that the murders of millions of people have followed in its wake.[42] Why is it they have not been able to stop that movement of the great red dragon?

It is because they have not bent the knee to confess the incarnation of the Woman in themselves, in the sons and daughters of God, in Mother Mary, and in the great examples who have gone before us. It is the Mother energy that comes to overthrow the tyrants. And without this energy, all of the dear people, all of the wonderful souls who are attempting to save our nation and do something about the insidious nature and the subtlety of this serpentine logic are not able to shatter the concepts, the logic of the fallen ones.

It takes the action of the Holy Ghost, which is the bride of

---

* The rod of Aaron is a symbol of the Mother light raised on the spine through the seven chakras. That energy becomes such a power as to be an instrument for the control and flow of energy, Spirit and Matter, in civilization. Exodus 7 describes how at Pharaoh's court, Moses cast down the rod of Aaron, which turned into a serpent. Pharaoh's sorcerers then cast down their rods. These also turned into serpents, but these were all swallowed up by the rod of Aaron. The power of the rod of Aaron is seen in Revelation 19:15, which says that the Manchild shall "rule all nations with a rod of iron."

the Virgin in you. You may have the Father, and you may have the Son as Lawgiver and Christ consciousness and as your I AM Presence and Christ Self, but you must pay the full price of surrender to pass the initiations to have the Holy Ghost dwell in you bodily, to receive those nine gifts of the Holy Spirit and to be a fountain of purity of the Mother flame.

If you are determined to be in the flame of the Mother and the flame of Shiva to destroy the lie that is destroying the people of this earth, then you must make that sacrifice. You must be willing to have stripped from your being the subtle lies into which you yourself have entered, which are the compromise of the energies of the love of the Holy Spirit and the purity of Mother.

Now let us see how this particular lie of the dialectic has woven itself in and out of world thought through the centuries.

Socrates and Plato

Socrates, one of the great philosophers of Ancient Greece, used a method of teaching based upon the dialectic, discussion, and dialogue. This method is summarized by Aristotle in the statement that "virtue is knowledge." Socrates' thinker is in search of only more and more abstract thought.

In Socrates' endless dialogues, we see that to him thoughts are considered "cosmic" simply because they are thought. Socrates believed that his wisdom lay in recognition of his ignorance. His intention was to convince others of their ignorance and lead them to knowledge through systematic human questioning. Socrates demanded of Athenian youth rigid mental training, in contrast to Pythagoras' mystery school at Crotona, where initiates pursued the development of the intuitive faculties of the heart.[43]

Plato, a student of Socrates, used the dialectic to confirm mathematical sciences and to do away with their hypothetical character. He presented his theory of dialectic to initiates who had successfully completed ten years of pure mathematics. Plato inherited from Socrates the application of dialectic to moral ideas, a mental process that he believed could lead the disciple to the realization of the nature of goodness.

If you read Socrates' dialogues that have been recorded and Plato's *Republic,* you find a most interesting process, one which feels most creative. It is the process of asking a question and the answer being another question and another question, until the obvious conclusion becomes the synthesis.

Socrates, Plato, and Aristotle are considered mighty men

and the foundation of Western philosophy. But there is a subtlety in the belief that we can arrive at absolute Truth by human knowledge, that by human knowledge and human questioning there can be a synthesis of that human knowledge, or that human ignorance, and that out of this synthesis absolute Truth can be born.

This is the lie of the Serpent. Something cannot come out of nothing. The evolution of Truth has its origin in the threefold flame, in the Christ consciousness. In order to be of that vibration, our consciousness must originate in that vibration. The only answer to human questioning is the answer that comes out of the Christ mind, and that is the Word. That Word dissolves the human question. It transmutes it; it doesn't answer it. Human logic upon human logic upon human logic can only equal human logic.

Somehow we are always thinking that if we have human goodness, we will get to God-goodness. But Jesus rejected that idea when he said, "Why callest thou me good? there is none good ... but God."[44] Jesus did not want people entering into a relative good and believing that through relative good they could arrive at absolute Good. There is only one Good: it is the Christ consciousness in you.

Kant and Hegel

While studying at the University of Berlin between the years 1836 and 1841, Karl Marx was introduced to Plato's dialectic as it had been interpreted by Immanuel Kant and Georg Wilhelm Friedrich Hegel. Kant's "Transcendental Dialectic" results in the belief that orthodox religion requires faith in a doctrine that human reason cannot justify. Kant maintained that Jesus originally taught a rational morality, a theology adapted to the reason of all men.

Kant's antipathy to what he considered speculative metaphysics and the hypothetical imperatives of Christian faith was initially accepted by Hegel, who wrote an interpretation of the Gospel according the Kantian ethics. Two or three years later, however, after careful study of Greek philosophy as well as an investigation of modern politics and economics, Hegel rejected Kant.

Hegel's perspective on Christian origins became that of a historian inspired by the doctrine of the Holy Spirit. To Hegel the spirit of man, his reason, cannot be subject to the limitations that Kant imposed upon it. Hegel believed that Jesus taught the understanding and the fulfillment of the law, not by Kantian rationalism (the justification of the law by the human mind) but by the love of God. As Paul said, "Love is the fulfilling of the law."[45] Kant believed that if reason attempted to go beyond the finite appearance world, it became lost in insoluble contradictions; whereas Hegel found in love a union of opposites, human and divine, and the transcendence of their seeming contradiction.

Immanuel Kant (1724–1804)

This is also a very important point, because we see in the understanding of Jesus Christ—the Son of man and the Son of God—that God himself could incarnate within the individual. But in fact, it is not the human and the divine in a certain sense of that word. It is the understanding that Spirit and Matter, body and soul, man is the totality of the expression of God. In other words, our very humanness in the divine sense is our divinity.

Jesus Christ is not a contradiction of the Infinite coming within the finite. Our perception of the finite must be altered. This living temple, this living soul must be recognized as also the totality and the fullness of Spirit. When it is the fullness of the manifestation of the flame that incarnates it, this brings life to the Matter spheres.

A central concept in Hegel's philosophy was what he called *Geist*, meaning "consciousness, mind, or Spirit."* Hegel's use of that word is indicative of his departure from atheistic rationalism, which is the rationale of Serpent. Hegel believed

---

* The word *Geist* is the etymological origin of the word *ghost*, but this term has lost much of its original meaning in English. Analogous words in other languages are the Greek *pneuma*, Latin *spiritus*, and Sanskrit *prana*. One element of the breadth of the original meaning in English is found in the term *Holy Ghost*.

Georg Wilhelm Friedrich Hegel
(1770–1831)

that since Spirit alone can comprehend Spirit, it is only because man *is* Spirit that he can receive the revelation of God.

Hegel's own mind transcended itself. He went from the point of the human mind to the utter realization that the reality of a person was the Spirit, was *Geist*, was consciousness; and only that point of reality could become and put on and incarnate the Word. Only God can become God. Only God-good can evolve God-good.

Hegel believed that what makes the universe intelligible is the understanding of it as an eternal cycle wherein Spirit comes to know itself as Spirit. This is precisely the truth.

When I studied these philosophers in college and I meditated upon certain glimmers of absolute Truth that they had come upon, I could feel the bursting of Christ consciousness. And then I could feel it covered over again by a wave of human reason. I was always impressed with the fact that Hegel arrived at this point.

This Spirit knowing of itself as Spirit comes through logic, through nature, and through mind-Spirit, or *Geist*. Hegel saw logic as positive, pure Spirit. He saw nature as the negative creation of Spirit that bears the mark of its Creator, in other words, as Matter. He saw Spirit coming to know Spirit through Alpha, through Omega, through the masculine and feminine polarity of a universe, and then through what he called *Geist* —self-consciousness, self-expression in history, self-discovery in art, religion, and philosophy. That *Geist*, then, becomes the individual Christ Self positioned in the midst of the Spirit-Matter being that you are, here and now.

Hegel believed that thinking always proceeded according to the dialectic pattern. The initial positive thesis is immediately negated by its antithesis, and further thought produces a synthesis, which again produces an antithesis. The process continues, but not indefinitely, for it is circular. The culmination is the Absolute, the return of thought to its Source, or to Spirit. What causes this cyclic process? Hegel explains that it is the power of the negative inherent within the positive: thought itself.

The ascended masters' teachings say exactly the same thing. We say Alpha contains Omega. We say Spirit contains Matter and that they are one. We say that the thesis is God the Father, the first polarity of being. The antithesis is God the Mother, which is contained in the thesis. The synthesis of the two is the Christ consciousness, and it is a point of the individualization of that God flame that transcends the prior thesis and antithesis.

The Christ Child, the Manchild fusing the light of Alpha and Omega, in each incarnation transcends its predecessor. It transcends that mind of God out of which it was created. Therefore you have an expanding cosmos. You have a self-transcending cosmos. You have a God who is continually transcending itself through this very act of creation—creating, preserving, and consummating. *Consummation* is the word for the Destroyer when there is nothing to destroy, so it is fulfillment or synthesis.

Here we see the cycles of life becoming life through this Trinity: Father the thesis, Mother the antithesis, and the synthesis being the fruit of the Christ and the fruit of the Holy

Spirit. The Serpent's dialectic and Marx's dialectic are a perversion of this basic cycle.

Hegel's system was based upon scientific, historical, theological, and philosophical investigation. His historical and political works elaborate an otherwise abstract dialectic theory. In his *Philosophy of Right,* Hegel describes a social and political order which satisfies the demands of both universal law and individual conscience—freedom without license. According to Hegel, such a state rests on the family and the guild. The guild is the cooperation of those who are engaged in a particular trade. Through cooperation with others, the individual finds satisfaction of his needs and recognizes the state, not as an alien oppressor but as the guardian of peace and order. Such a state, unlike any existing in Hegel's day, was a limited monarchy with parliamentary government and trial by jury.

Hegel's philosophy reveals his conviction that history is the course of mankind's advance towards self-knowledge—Spirit as Spirit. The goal of civilization was for the individual through his *Geist*, his consciousness—what we would call his Christ consciousness—to come to know himself as God. According to Hegel, history is the fulfillment of God's purpose: freedom. *Geist* is free in essence. The Spirit has free will. The task, then, of we who live upon earth is to build institutions in which man can express that freedom.

Feuerbach and the Rise of Rationalism

Karl Marx is known as a Neo-Hegelian, one who comes after Hegel and reinterprets his philosophy. At the University of Berlin, where Hegel held the chair of philosophy, Marx was drawn into speculative quarrels over the meaning of the complex Hegelian dialectic.

Hegel, limited though he might have been as an individual, was used to set forth once again the basic premise of the true logic of the Christ mind, presented in the Garden of Eden by the Guru Maitreya. Now comes Marx quarreling over the meaning of it, disputing with it, arguing about it. Marx accepts Hegel's theory of dialectic evolution with one fundamental variance: Marx denies the existence of Spirit as the original thesis, as the essence of the antithesis, and as the unifying factor of the synthesis.

Although Marx was fascinated by the Hegelian dialectic, he was determined to put it "back on its feet." Marx translated Hegel's idealistic thesis of pure Spirit into a rationalistic thesis that he called the "productive man," *homo faber*.* Marx's comment in a series of epigrams "On Hegel" stressed Hegel's supposed "opaqueness and ambiguity": "Words I [Marx] teach all mixed up into a devilish muddle. Thus anyone may think just what he chooses to think."[46]

---

* *Homo faber*: Latin, literally "man the maker." The term is used in Roman literature to refer to man's ability to control his destiny. It is sometimes contrasted with *Homo adorans*, "worshipping man." In Judeo-Christian philosophy the purpose of man is to worship God, whereas for Marx, the purpose of man was for what he could produce.

Ludwig Andreas von Feuerbach (1804–1872) Feuerbach's embrace of materialism had a great influence on Karl Marx.

Marx was greatly influenced by Ludwig Feuerbach, who saw in Hegel's philosophy "something extremely revolutionary." However, Feuerbach took Hegel's philosophy in an even more revolutionary direction, a break with religion, "a transition from idealism to materialism." To Feuerbach, man is the "real secret of religion." Traditional doctrine maintains that "God created man in his own image. Feuerbach maintains the reverse: man has created God in his own image."[47]

This is precisely what Lucifer did. Lucifer rejected God as God and said, "This is what God really is. He's incapable of doing his job." Lucifer created a god made in his own image and likeness. And all of the fallen ones who follow after him come up with this same philosophy. They make fun of organized religion. They say there is no God, and all of these silly little people who believe in God have simply created a god to take care of their needs and wants.

Feuerbach says that "there is no supersensual knowledge as religion and philosophy maintain.... Knowledge of the world is possible only on the basis of sense experience."[48] Proof of anything must be existential, experimental. It must come from the five senses. This is the utter degradation of the faculty of the Christ consciousness and the senses of the soul of the sons and daughters of God. And yet this empirical method—proving by the senses—is put upon us, especially in our universities and colleges. We are taught that this is the only way to think, the only way to draw conclusions in science or religion or any other subject.

This is a very heavy lie, and anyone who goes against empiricism is considered as not having been liberated from earlier centuries where faith guided men's activities in the absence of science. There is disdain, criticism, condemnation, and judgment of our youth who would even dare to approach the intuitive faculties of the heart and to use them to perceive God. However, only Spirit can perceive Spirit. Only Spirit can know Spirit. And therefore, if we are ever to know what is Real, it is the Real in us which must perceive it, not the faculties of the senses perceiving the unreal cosmos.

Feuerbach repeated the philosophy of the rationalist, which was in vogue in that century. In *The Essence of Christianity,* he maintained that although Hegel had discovered that man was God in a dialectic state of becoming, he had not taken the logical next step in concluding that God is man: *Homo homini Deus est* ("Man is God to man"),[49] i.e., that man imposes the idea of God upon whatever is most sublime in mankind.

Feuerbach believed that it was not belief in God that created this state but doubt of his existence, that Christianity alienated man by depriving him of his political energy. He saw man as a political animal who creates his god, his figures who are world leaders, and he worships them. In fact if man created God, then obviously man must be God.[50]

This is the Satanic enthroning of the carnal mind. The only difference between Satanism and the way of the Christ is who is enthroned in the temple. The carnal mind and its elevation to the plane of the heart is Satanism. The Christ mind elevated and adored and worshiped is the teaching of Christ. Here again we have a mixture; we have a synthesis of those two religions. Unfortunately, Christianity today is a mixture of the doctrines of Satan and Jesus Christ.

I am determined that illumined sons and daughters of God will be able to undo, thread by thread, truth and error wherever it is found. I give you this understanding so that I do not need to tell you what is light and what is darkness. You will know. You will have the sword of the Spirit and the great Word of the living God, and you will penetrate by the Logos. It will become obvious to you within your own temple when you are serving Satan and the carnal mind and when you are serving the Lord Christ.

Saint Germain and Jesus Christ bring the ascended masters' teachings today because the people are in a mass ignorance concerning these most important points of the Law.

The X-ing Out of the Trinity

In 1846 Karl Marx wrote a description of German philosophy at that time:

> According to the reports of our ideologists, Germany has, during the last decade, undergone a revolution of unexampled proportions ... a revolution in comparison with which the French Revolution was mere child's play. With unbelievable rapidity one empire was supplanted by another, one mighty hero was struck down by another still bolder and more powerful in the universal chaos. During three years, from 1842 to 1845, Germany went through a cataclysm more violent in character than anything which had happened in any previous century. All this, if it is true, took place only in the region of pure thought. For we are dealing with a remarkable phenomenon—the decomposition of Absolute Spirit.
>
> When the last spark of life disappeared from its body, its various constituents disintegrated and entered into new combinations and formed new substances. Dealers in philosophy, who had previously made a living by exploiting the Absolute Spirit, now threw themselves avidly on the new combinations. Each busily began to dispose of his share of it.[51]

From his rationalistic thesis, Marx evolved a rationalistic antithesis. Nature, which Hegel identified as the essential antithesis (and which we understand as the Mother principle) produced for Marx continual conflict with his thesis of the "productive man." By denying the inherent Spirit which Hegel found within nature, Marx made human nature the antithesis of the productive man. Human nature created by the rational will is obedient only to so-called rational laws, in contrast to the irrational law of love.

Marx perceives the interaction of his thesis and antithesis as illimitable class struggle. His synthesis is not Hegelian transcendence, but death and destruction. He doesn't see Spirit transcending itself, becoming more and more of God—God becoming more and more of God. He always sees synthesis as death and destruction. And that is where the fallen ones have determined to take the cycles of the Trinity: to x-out each member of the Trinity, to x-out and pervert its cycles, and to create not eternal life, not the ascension, but death.*

World Communism in its very origins and inceptions, as far back as Lemuria, has been the culture of death that is anti-Mother. The culture of the Woman and her seed is the culture of life. Mother is the fountain of life, the fountain of the ascension flame. The ascension flame rising is the buoying up of the soul and the returning of that soul, in the joy of the Lord, to the fullness of Reality, the ascended master state.

All of the fallen ones knew exactly why God created the incarnate Word in his sons and daughters. It was so that they could go through the initiations of Spirit-Matter, master the universe, increase their God consciousness through their

---

* This aim is even seen symbolically in Marx's name. It begins with the *M* of Mother. The second letter, *A*, is for Alpha, or First Cause. *R* is a letter meaning ray—the ray of light. Wherever that *R* is manifest, it implies the manifestation of the Son. So we here have Mother, Father, and Son. At the end of the name, we find not the cosmic cross of white fire, but the *X*, the symbol of Satan canceling out the Trinity, crossing out the Christ in you. When you make the sign of the cross in the name of the Father, the Mother, the Son, and the Holy Spirit, you are marking the sign of the incarnation of the Word where you are, and you are defeating or dissolving the x-ing out of your soul and being that is practiced daily in black magic, in Satanism, and in the condemnation and the accusations of the "father of lies" (John 8:44). So the very name *Marx* is a warning that this individual has come for a single purpose: to x-out the Trinity in the sons and daughters of God.

Karl Marx (1818–1883)
Photograph from 1875

self-mastery, and then return Home with a net gain.

Remember the multiplication of the talent, the multiplication of the threefold flame. We must return back to God with an increased God consciousness. "My word shall not return unto me void."[52] My sons and daughters will return unto me in the fullness of my Spirit multiplied 100 percent. Each outbreath of the creation, which goes on for aeons, is followed by the great inbreath in which God, by the ascension spiral, draws all of us back into his heart. This becomes the great increase, the great harvest of the cosmos.

My little child said to me the other day, "Mommy, why did God send us out into the universe where the planets are? Was it so that we could help the people?" I could see the perception of the child, the self-awareness of origin, the memory of being one in the Father-Mother God, and all of a sudden realizing, "I am not in the Great Central Sun with Alpha and Omega. Why did God send us out here into that universe of Matter where the planets are?"

It was precisely so that we could help the people, so that we could increase God consciousness, so that we could bring back the net gain.

Conflict and Destruction

Marx believed that social progress is achieved only through conflict between old and new systems, and that "class struggle" is the great motive power of history.[53] In fact, what Marx said and his belief behind what he said are two different streams of consciousness.

Dialectical materialism is a rationale and a logic which ultimately, fundamentally, even Marx himself does not believe. He sets it forth to be that which will advance the highest human good. That is the lie. That is the bait for the children of God. He knows in the very core of his being that the end thereof is the way of death.*

Those who have been behind dialectical materialism have known exactly the end from the beginning: the destruction and the death of the souls of sons and daughters of God. Some know it consciously; some know it subconsciously. Some are tools; some are the originators of the lie.

The negative force which Hegel saw as inherent within the positive force and as the cause of its cyclic progress, Marx identifies in the social system as germs of its own destruction—reforms which ideally operate as a foreign body within an existing system to accelerate its death. Progress is impaired by limited reforms that prematurely reduce tension. To Marx, violence is the price to be paid for progress.

In other words, evils in society are not to be put out and destroyed. They are considered the antithesis of the thesis, a

---

* "There is a way that seemeth right unto a man and the end thereof are the ways of death" (Prov. 14:12).

very necessary part of the process. Evil should be allowed to grow and to become big so that it has its self-destructive force upon the entire society.

This is apparent today. The failure to check evils in our Western society is allowing them to become the antithesis of the culture of the Mother unto its destruction, creating a justification for the violence of those who then come and say: "We will deliver you from these evils of society. We will bring in our synthesis of that evil with the original premise and evolve a new form of government, a new form of an economy."

This is a very subtle matter. Instead of saying that plus and minus are one, Father-Mother God are one, thesis and antithesis are Spirit and Matter, it is saying that good and evil are one. This is one of the most fundamental lies of the Serpent: the denial of Mother, or Matter; the claim that it is not Matter, or Mother, who is in polarity with Spirit, or Father, but evil—misqualified Mother, maya.*

To Marxists, to dialectical materialists, evil becomes the polarity of good. This is one of those very basic lies. People talk about good and evil as opposites. But good and evil are not in polarity. Evil is unreal; good is Real. By God's consciousness and the Christ consciousness, we eliminate the necessity for evil as an integrating factor in our society. We eliminate the need for conditions of decay, corruption, destruction, violence, and terror in order to evolve a better society.

All of the destruction and mass murder and terrorism that follows in the wake of Marxist philosophy, all of this evolves out of Marx's premise, right out of these nineteenth-century philosophy books. And there you see the lie that it is necessary to do evil that good may come.[54]

You hear this same lie in New Age circles among any

---

* Maya [Sanskrit]: literally illusion, deception, appearance. Something created or fabricated, not ultimately real; the impermanent phenomenal world viewed as reality; the principle of relativity and duality by which the one Reality appears as the manifold universe. The ascended masters teach that maya is the veil of misqualified energy that man imposes upon Matter through his misuse of the sacred fire.

number of so-called gurus who will tell you that anything goes. They say that it doesn't matter what you are or what you do, that there is no standard, that there is no Law, that there is no Lawgiver, that there is no Father, Son, or Holy Spirit. They say that good and evil are a combination, and whatever part or facet of it you are expressing, it's ok because you can do your thing.

This is the lie. And we must watch this lie because it is the path that masses of God's children are following. Some follow it in religion, some follow it in politics, some in economics, some in culture, and some in education.

Five Economic Systems

In his *Communist Manifesto*, which Marx published in 1848, he distinguished five economic forms or modes of production: Primitive Communal, Slave, Feudal, Capitalistic, and Socialistic.

The *Manifesto* is a very short document. You must read it. You cannot refute the lie if you don't know the lie. Likewise, you must read the New Testament because you cannot refute the lie if you do not have the Word and the Christ consciousness.

Under the first of the five modes of production in the *Manifesto*, the Primitive Communal, the means of production are socially owned. Under the second, the slave owner owns them. Under the third, the feudal lord owns his men only partially, as they have some property. Under the fourth, the Capitalist owns the means of production, but not his men, whom he can no longer dispose of as he pleases even though they are compelled to work for him. Under the fifth mode, the Socialistic, which has not yet come into existence, the workers themselves will own the means of production, and with the abolition of the contradictions inherent in Capitalism, production will reach its fullest development.

According to the dialectic principle, every new stage takes up whatever was of value in that which it has negated, and each stage represents an advance upon its predecessor in both production and freedom. From the Primitive Communal to the Slave, the Feudal, the Capitalistic, and the Socialistic, each stage evolves inevitably out of the previous one.

The first edition of *The Communist Manifesto*, published in London, 1848

This is why Khrushchev said, "We will bury you!"[55] He believed in dialectical materialism as a philosophy of history. These fallen ones do believe that history is on their side and that the conclusion is inevitable because of the logic of dialectical materialism. They believe in a logic—it happens to be the logic of the Serpent.

We believe in the Logos, the Word incarnate, but we do not understand the logical conclusions of the Word incarnate, so we are not as certain of our victory. We have not organized under that Logos as free people, as free men and women throughout the world. We are not as understanding of our Logos as the fallen ones are of their diabolical logic.

Millions of Communists today, many of whom are children of the light, believe in the inevitability of the logical conclusion of something that is mere theory. It has never even been proven that dialectical materialism is true or that it works.* It is a complete lie and perversion of the cycles of the Trinity.

Someone has to tell them the truth. We can give the message and we can publish the books, but someone has to tell them heart to heart. And that someone is you. It is sons and daughters of God. It is all of us. This is the message that must unfold.

---

* One obvious failure of Marxist theory is that it predicted that the nations with the wealthiest and most advanced Capitalist systems would be the first to fall to Communism, as oppressed factory workers rose up in revolution. In fact, the first Communist revolution was in Russia, which was in 1917 still a largely agricultural economy. Russia did not abolish the feudal system until the reforms of Alexander II in 1861, hundreds of years after other European nations. Subsequent Communist revolutions have also occurred in poor agricultural nations, not in the wealthy Capitalist nations as Marx predicted.

Class Warfare

Marx saw the separate stages of social progress as each represented by a social class. Feudalism is represented by the nobility. Capitalism is represented by the entrepreneurs, which he called the *bourgeoisie*, a term he uses with great disdain.* He looks down upon the Capitalistic enterprise. He looks down upon the shopkeeper, the one who owns something and therefore is the foundation of the free-enterprise system. Finally, Socialism is represented by the workers, the proletariat.† Marx maintained that the victory of the new class cannot be limited by a democracy that substitutes ballots for bullets and that requires respect for inalienable rights.

In the class struggle that Marx witnessed following the Industrial Revolution, he professed extreme sympathy for the injured and the insulted laboring masses. This sympathy for the downtrodden characterizes this entire philosophy. The sympathy originates in the sympathy of the Devil for himself: "Feel sorry for me. I have been kicked out of heaven. God has denied me his light, his bread, his energy, his consciousness.

---

* *Bourgeoisie*, from the Old French *bourgeois*, literally a "town dweller." Before the French Revolution they were a class between the peasants and the landed aristocracy, town dwellers who were able to accumulate personal wealth through a trade or business. In contemporary usage, the term is used to describe the ruling class in Capitalist societies, and more broadly the middle class.
† *Proletariat*, from Latin *proletarius*, "producing offspring," used in ancient Rome to refer to freedmen, including artisans and small tradesmen, who were not wealthy and whose primary contribution to the state was providing offspring who could serve in the legions or colonize new territories. In Marxist philosophy the term is used to refer to those who do not own capital or the means of production and who earn their living by selling their labor. *The Communist Manifesto* concludes with Marx's famous statement, "The proletarians have nothing to lose but their chains. They have a world to win. Working men of all countries, unite!"

Now give me what God has failed to give me."

That does not mean that the sons and daughters of God do not have utter compassion for those who are without, those who are the poor in spirit. But feeling sorry for those who do not earn by the path of initiation that which it is their right to earn is the emotion that enters in and engenders the fervor of World Communism—sympathy for the fallen ones.

Who are the "injured and the insulted laboring masses"? I have lived in this country all my life. I know hundreds if not thousands of working people who love their work, who do not consider themselves injured and insulted by the owners of the businesses or the corporations for which they work.

So beware of theory. There are many terms in this theory that are simply value judgments, that exist as concepts floating in the air, that don't have any relationship to real life. Who is the man in the street? That's another concept. Who is the typical person who represents the masses? Who are the masses? People are not masses. They are individuals. And when you get to know people individual by individual, there is no such thing as the masses. There are souls evolving Godward, and you can't lump them into this mass, the proletariat.

Marx promised that violent repression of the Capitalists by the worker would ultimately result in the dictatorship of the proletariat, the dictatorship of the working class. This Marxist synthesis is an inanimate economic system in which technology is used to obtain increasing control of nature—inanimate because Spirit is not the thesis, and the antithesis is likewise devoid of the Spirit. Instead of the Hegelian synthesis, *Geist*, there is mere mind, mechanized mind. Mechanization man is the goal of dialectical materialism.* According to dialectic law Marx's synthesis should return man to thesis, "productive man." But en route he produces not transcendence but death and destruction.

Reminiscent of Feuerbachian ethics, Marx's economic

---

* The end of this path is spelled out by Saint Paul: "To be carnally minded is death" (Rom. 8: 6–10).

interpretation of history, or economic determinism, proposes that religion, patriotism, and all other so-called idealistic feelings are the product of economic conditions and their effect upon the human mind—in other words, that Spirit is the creation of Matter. Marx felt that history was on his side, that history was predetermined, and this predestination without God was reduced to simply the interplay of these forces in society, without a ruling mind, without these forces serving a mind—either a mind of God or the mind of the people.

The Great White Brotherhood teaches us that there is no predestination. The Brotherhood champions free will because God has set free will. This means there is no predestination of golden ages, dark ages, or the pattern of history. We are not robots, mechanical beings following a mechanical economic determinism. We are God-free beings with a flame in the heart, intended to be free to apply the laws of a cosmos, all of which are supportive of individual freedom.

In the absolute sense, God never brings man to a state of slavery in order to bring him to future freedom. In the relative sense, man brings himself to that state by his own self-imposed laws of limitation. And if man has brought himself to a state of slavery, this does not mean that we can conclude that by dialectical materialism he will evolve out of slavery through economic determinism. This is impossible. Man evolves out of slavery through Christ, through the liberation of the soul that is a burst of consciousness, that is the elevation of that Christ in the temple of being.

We can obviously see that history has followed these steps. But this has not happened according to the interpretation of Marx. This evolution has been the result of karma—the karma of ignorance of the law of the individual Christ. It was not necessary to go through these stages. These were not dependent on one another. They did not come out of this dialectic.

They came out of the fact that one by one, step by step, the individual was evolving a Christ consciousness, and therefore he gained a greater and greater enlightenment of the law of economics set forth by Jesus Christ and the flow of the abundant life. And the greatest example of that abundant life in the guru-chela relationship is found in the free-enterprise system.[56] That is the evolution of the Christ consciousness by the cycles of Alpha and Omega, as thesis, antithesis, and synthesis of the Christ within us.

The fallen ones can take history, they can take any subject or any field and superimpose upon it the logic of the carnal mind. And if you do not know the facts and the figures of this process of evolution, and if you don't have at your side the rod and the scepter of authority of the Christ mind, you cannot refute that logic. You cannot see that working through the evolution of man in God and God in man has been the Christ principle that is the foundation.

Following Marx's logic, Socialism should be the next phase of economic determinism after Capitalism. However, it is not. Socialism is and ever has been the fallen state of man and woman. And what the fallen ones are trying to take from us with this logic is the foundation of the golden-age economy.

The fallen ones are trying to return us to the most primitive form of life and living on earth. The most ancient cultures have their foundation in Socialism. Socialism was never born in the 1850s. It has been around as the subtle lie within the being of man for centuries.*

---

*Russian dissident Igor Shafarevich has explained that the world's first Socialist states were the first states of any kind and that Socialism has existed over the entire span of human history. "Socialism cannot be linked with a specific area, geographical context, or culture. All its features, familiar to us from contemporary experience, are met in various historical, geographical and cultural conditions: in socialist states we observe the abolition of private ownership of the means of production, state control of everyday life, and the subordination of the individual to the power of the bureaucracy." Shafarevich cites three ancient socialist states: Mesopotamia in the twenty-second and twenty-first centuries BC, the Old Kingdom of Egypt, and the Incas. All were characterized by lack of private property, a large bureaucracy, a centrally directed economy, and a forced labor system which tended to weaken the family structure. They reveal, in the slavery of the entire population and the extreme regimentation, the descent into which people who had once lived in golden ages fell with the sinking of Lemuria and Atlantis. See Igor Shafarevich, "Socialism in Our Past and Future," in Alexander Solzhenitsyn et al., *From Under the Rubble* (New York: Little, Brown and Company, 1975).

Dialectical Materialism

In collaboration with Friedrich Engels, Marx wrote a voluminous critique entitled *The Holy Family*, which first appeared in 1832. In this work, Marx and Engels formulated the method of their economic interpretation of history based on the proposition that the mode of production in material life determines the general character of the social, political, and spiritual processes of life.

Marx and Engels proposed that it is not the consciousness of man that determines their existence—on the contrary, their social existence determines people's consciousness. The environment makes the individual. The environment is essentially economic, and therefore, Marx and Engels say, whatever form of economic system surrounds us molds our being, our thinking, and our outlook.

We can agree that it is partially true that the environment we grow up in determines the way we think. But it does not determine the total being and identity of man. And it is not able to discolor the basic and inherent truth of the flow of the abundant life within us.

According to Marx, production forces and production relations form the infrastructure or foundation for the entire social superstructure of ideas, institutions, law, politics, moral and religious concepts, as well as cultural standards and artistic expression. This superstructure inevitably changes with the evolution of the infrastructure of the economic system. How? Through dialectic.

Marx's economic interpretation of history, which he called

Friedrich Engels (1820–1895)
Engels came from a wealthy family
and supported Marx financially. Marx
and Engels were co-authors of *The
Communist Manifesto.*

historical materialism, is founded upon his interpretation of dialectic, which he therefore called *dialectic materialism*—the evolution of history, economics, or government through the dialogue, the system of thesis, antithesis, and synthesis. You might say that the term *dialectic materialism* is therefore the dialogue of the materialist.

Marx was convinced that social and historical processes followed the law of dialectical materialism, which he said was no less universal than the laws of physics and chemistry. Or one could say that he employed this rationale as bait for God's children, whom he would dupe into implementing their own self-destruction through his system, which was based on the philosophy of Satan.

It is not important whether Marx knew the full ramifications of Satanism behind his work, because those who spawn the lie know the end from the beginning. It is not necessary to prove whether or not Marx was in fact consciously in league with the powers of darkness, because the subconscious mind is enough to determine the totality of the consciousness of the individual.

Marx said that guided by the law of dialectical materialism, mankind would achieve a utopian society. Marx knew that a utopian society was unattainable, but he used the concept to perpetuate endless class struggle and the Socialist revolution, destroying bodies, souls, and minds through murder, war, and terrorism.

Marx believed that the mere existence of any institution proved that it was rational and even desirable, because whether good or evil, just or unjust, it was nevertheless a necessary step in human progress. However, to say that everything in society —from crime to any form of institution—is desirable and necessary, merely because it exists is to throw out the entire tradition of the teachings of the Great White Brotherhood from Zoroaster to Gautama to Confucius to Lao-tzu to Jesus Christ to our modern saints. This, in fact, is exactly what Marx did. It is exactly what Lenin did. And it is exactly what the Communist state does today. By throwing out the teachings of the Brotherhood, it throws out the path of initiation.

When there is no path of initiation upon a planetary body, the reason for being of that planetary body ceases. That is the state in which the earth once was—an entire planetary body, an entire lifewave, was devoid of the memory of the great God flame that burns upon the altar of the heart. In that hour, because the path was lost, because not one soul was achieving Christhood, the Cosmic Council decreed the dissolution of earth and her evolutions. It was at that moment that the Lord Sanat Kumara, the Ancient of Days, appeared before the Cosmic Council and said, "Wait, I will go to earth. I will keep the flame of life. I will restore the Christ consciousness and the path of evolution, the path of initiation."[57]

How did the people of this planetary body reach that low estate? The ancient record reveals that that point of destruction of God's self-awareness was reached through the exact same subtlety of the lie of the Serpent—precisely through dialectical materialism, a diabolical Socialism, an atheistic Communism. It is an ancient lie spawned upon planetary body after planetary body for the destruction of the soul through the x-ing out of the Trinity. For hundreds of thousands of years we have been striving to draw mankind back to that God-awareness. And now the very same lie has been repeated in recent centuries, organized, put forth into a diabolical system that now holds vast sections of the earth under its dominion.*

Now we must come once again and learn the basic truths of how it all happened, because we too, from time to time, have been swallowed up in the mists of maya—Mother energy misqualified. In Genesis we read that "there went up a mist from the earth, and it covered the whole face of the ground." That mist was maya, the logic of the Serpent, *mist-ification*, misqualification of the true creation of sons and daughters of God after the image and likeness of Elohim.†

This misuse of ascension's flame produces smog, maya, unclear seeing, unclear thinking. And suddenly we have lost hold of the thread of *righteousness*, the *right use* of the Law and the *right use* of the Logos. This is something to ponder when you are trying to determine, "What am I doing here on this planet? Why was I born? What did I come for? And what is this big mess we are all in?"

It is just a matter of waking up. When they asked Gautama Buddha what made him different, he said, "I am awake." He perceived that all of the rest of us had fallen asleep to our original vow, fallen asleep to our original awareness and our reason for coming to earth. He was the first to realize that he was awake in contrast to all others, who were asleep.

---

* In 1980, more than a third of the world's population lived under governments espousing Communist doctrines, including the Warsaw Pact nations of Eastern Europe, the Soviet Union, and the People's Republic of China.
† The first chapter of Genesis describes how "God created man in his own image, in the image of God [*Elohim* in the original Hebrew] created he him; male and female created he them." The "mist from the earth" is described in Genesis 2:6. The following verse describes a second creation of man: "And the LORD God formed man of the dust of the ground, and breathed into his nostrils the breath of life; and man became a living soul."

The Force of Anti-Mother

Dialectical materialism is in itself not valid according to the teachings of the Brotherhood, because it bases the cause-effect sequences in society upon the phases of the human consciousness—the reaction of new phases to old and then mixing the two together producing a new product that is still the human consciousness. This is what is written in scripture, "ever learning but never coming to the knowledge of the truth."[58] In fact, dialectical materialism is a *diabolical* materialism because it neglects the definition of Matter as Mother and the alchemy of the Mother in civilization as the *Mater-realization* of the God flame by sons and daughters of the Most High.

There is a difference between materialism and Mater-realization. When you realize the fullness of the Mother flame, you have all of the accoutrements of civilization, of Matter, the crystallization of the God flame. There is nothing wrong with Matter. Matter was never inherently evil. That's the Big Lie, that Matter is evil. Matter has always been Mother. Mother has always been the abundance of the light. And Mater-realization is what we are about.

We, as Americans, should not be accused of being materialists simply because God has given us the alchemy to draw down a civilization and a technology. We should not be accused of hoarding the wealth of the world and having more goods than anyone else. That is our Christ-attainment and it is ours to have as an attainment as a nation, and it is ours to bequeath upon other nations. But by the law of the path of initiation and of hierarchy, our abundance is not ours to give away to those who have failed to bend the knee and confess Father, Son, Holy Spirit, and Mother flame.

Materialism without the Mother is anti-Mother, anti-Matter. Dialectical materialism itself is anti-Mother. You have heard of Antichrist. There is also the force of anti-Mother, and it is manifest today in World Communism enslaving and murdering the children of Alpha and Omega. They are being persecuted, brutally treated, and slaughtered this very hour. This is anti-Mother, the murdering of the Mother, because the Matter temple is Mother. And in this temple the Christ is intended to be born.

You are the key to the incarnation of God to the evolutions of this earth. And God is incarnating every day in the bursting of the God consciousness in you. And we will no longer allow this slaughter of the holy innocents and the martyrdom of the saints at the hand of Herod's men. This has to stop. And it will stop by the power of God in you. It will stop because the LORD God has decreed it so. He has willed it so. And we as sons and daughters of God have decreed it so and willed it so, because we are the echo of his life. It's not because man wills it so. It is because God wills it so.

Let us remember the premise of our logic. Upon that premise and upon that logic, the history of cosmos is on *our* side. And it is preordained because *we will choose by free will to ordain it* as God has ordained it.

First Cause

The process of Mater-realization cannot be confined to a rationalist, dialectic synthesis, because it is the evolutionary process of the soul through its integration with Truth, not error; with absolute Spirit, not the relativity of mortal law, mortal mind, and mortal cause-effect sequences. The root of the word *mortal* is *mort*, which means "death." So the mortal man is the death-man. The man who is subject to death is not the God-man.

Dialectic materialism looks at life as a human evolution, instead of seeing that there are inner causes behind outer manifestations. But there is the law of First Cause (your own great causal body, your own I AM THAT I AM), which sets in motion the Word, the individual Christ Self that must become flesh in the sons and daughters of God through the great synthesis of the Mother flame. That soul must descend and must put on those coats of skins,* those four lower bodies that are necessary for life in the Matter spheres. And there is the law of secondary causes set in motion by the free will of man, the freewill expressions of the soul once it has descended.

The First Cause, which is God's karma, is the descent of the soul with free will. Under that First Cause, obedient to that will, endued with that wisdom, filled with that Holy Spirit love,

---

* Genesis 3:21 describes how God provides "coats of skins" for Adam and Eve after their fall. This is a symbol for the clothing of the soul in the bodies that would be needed outside of the Mystery School of Eden, in the dense octaves below the heaven world. These are the etheric body, the mental body, the emotional (or astral) body, and the physical body. These are known as the four lower bodies, in contrast to the three aspects of the purely spiritual being of man: the Holy Christ Self, the causal body, and the I AM Presence.

we can manifest God-mastery. Disobedient to First Cause, entering the *ignore-ance* of the Law and the anti-love synthesis, we then set up secondary causes.

When you analyze history and life on earth, you must be able to determine what is First Cause (God), and what are the secondary causes—cause-effect sequences in manifestation. One is God's karma—Good. The other is man's karma—relative good and evil. When you look at life though the single eye of the All-Seeing Eye of God, you easily see the separation of this water and oil. You see that your native origin and your destiny, your beginning and your ending, is First Cause. Out of God we come forth; unto God we return. That is Reality.

Secondary causes are temporarily real. They are real because we sustain them by free will, but they are unreal in the absolute sense, and therefore we do not feed them energy. We cut them from the vine of life, and we put them into the fiery furnace where the tares belong. We put that negative karma into the sacred fire, into the violet flame, and it is consumed. If it were Real, it could not be consumed. The only thing Real about it is God's energy that was used to create it. This energy must return to him stripped of the secondary cause-effect sequences.

What is true of the individual is also true of civilization. There is First Cause: golden-age civilizations, golden-age God-government and economy. There are secondary cause-effect sequences: the karma of a society and a civilization that is not founded upon the Rock of Christ.

This law of karma that we have set in motion has no inevitable conclusions; it only has the perpetual process of resolution by the law of love and its transmutative sacred fire. The agents of this transmutation are always the Word made flesh and the fiery baptism of the Holy Ghost. This process continues until the Absolute is attained, that is, until the soul's liberation from all cause-effect sequences—dialectic, didactic, or materialistic—through integration with the law of the One, or the I AM THAT I AM.

Transmutation is the real science of the Mother, not a dialectical materialism whereby things keep superseding each other toward an imagined goal. The real science of the Mother is transmutation, because it is transcendence. The thesis and the synthesis must have that sacred-fire transmutation in order to evolve to a higher plane of being. The science of transmutation is the freeing of energy. That is true evolution—Spirit-Matter evolution.

That is the way out of the Gordian knot of human karma, cause-effect sequences. There is no way out through economic determinism because it is always subject to the law of death—mortality.

Instead of dialectical materialism, we pursue Matter-realization through the transmutation of the Holy Ghost, the sacred fire, the fiery baptism. Inherent in that is the judgment and the cleaving asunder of the Real from the unreal. God is the answer. And this is the Word, the Logos, swallowing up human reason.

The Finite and the Infinite

Christ does not give human answers to human questions. Christ is the consuming light, the love, the love-light that is perpetual resolution. Day by day we are evolving. We are revolving about the sun center of being. Day by day we are transcending the former self, but it is not by the process of dialectical materialism. This is what all the world must know in order to be free from the dragon.

> Humpty Dumpty sat on a wall,
> Humpty Dumpty had a great fall;
> All the king's horses and all the king's men
> Couldn't put Humpty together again.

Can you put Humpty Dumpty back together again?

The Humpty Dumpty story is very interesting because it illustrates that the Absolute is not attained by a synthesis of the parts of the whole, but by the transcendence of the parts.

The apostle Paul stated this principle of the finite not becoming the Infinite but giving way to it by transmutation, the alchemy of the Holy Ghost. Paul said, "This corruptible must put on incorruption, this mortal must put on immortality."[59] He said, "Flesh and blood cannot inherit the kingdom of God."[60]

Don't be too sure about putting Humpty Dumpty together again. Humpty Dumpty symbolizes the egg, or the "I," of the human ego. The human ego has its great fall. Lucifer had his great Fall. He's been trying to put things back together again ever since, but he's never been able to do so. You can't put the human ego back together again. The fragments of the not-self can never become the cosmic egg of the Divine Ego—not by a Hegelian synthesis or by a dialectical materialism.

Nevertheless, something cannot be created out of nothing. The broken fragments of the egg of the former self are the necessary elements that must be sacrificed in the alchemy of self-transcendence. By transmutation alone do they become the components of the Great Self. These elements—the broken eggshell, the yolk, the white, the whole mess sitting on the ground—are the sacrifice. It must be placed upon the altar of the heart and in the laboratory of the soul. That is the time and space consecrated to the rite, the ritual of change.

Here, in the heart, the threefold flame of the Father, the Son, and the Holy Spirit can do what all the king's horses and all the king's men can never do—put the Humpty Dumpty of the human consciousness back together again. They try to do this by the endless, inanimate, economic process of thesis, antithesis, and synthesis, which leads not to the absolute Good of the individual self-realized in God, but to the absolute Evil of the individual who is annihilated in a philosophy of nihilism.

Only through the Trinity can this broken egg, this broken fallen one, regain an identity. Then it becomes the cosmic egg of a cosmic consciousness; it becomes the Divine Ego. But then it is no longer the Humpty Dumpty, no longer the broken shells. Those must be transmuted.

When you come to the altar of God, you must have something to place upon it. That something is the sacrifice: the human will, the human intellect, the human ego, the human desire. It is broken. It can never become something—God. But it is that something that must be placed there. It is the coal out of which the diamond will be fashioned by the Trinity.

Don't try to make a chalice out of the broken fragments of your human consciousness. Let the human consciousness be put upon the Rock and be broken. Let the flame of the Christ rise through it to form and reform you in Christ. Let that energy misused be now transmuted, and let the Divine Egg appear.

The alternative is precisely what Marx's dialectical materialism and the fallen ones have been trying to do since the beginning. They have been trying to convince all of humanity that it is possible to put together a superior man, a superman, a superwoman, by the human components—and to do it without God.

Sympathy for the Devil

Dialectical materialism is the underlying rationale of the religion of Antichrist. World Communism is a religion of hatred based on a doctrine of social salvation through the synthesis of death, instead of through the integration of the Word. It is the invention of Satan himself.

Was Marx a Satanist? Was it all a pretense, this passionate sympathy for the injured and insulted laboring masses? The only injured and insulted one to benefit from Marxist doctrine is Satan himself. Marx's sympathy is for the Devil.

Karl Heinrich Marx was born on May 5, 1818, in the German Rhineland. His father, Herschel Marx, was a rich, well-respected lawyer and a disciple of Immanuel Kant. Although many of his ancestors were rabbis, Herschel held vaguely deist views and was officially received as a Lutheran "for convenience" just one year before Karl's birth, when the anti-Jewish laws of 1816 suddenly cut off his means of livelihood.

Karl had a sharp and lucid mind, a stubborn and domineering temper, and a turbulent love of indulgence. At the prestigious University of Berlin, Marx was tempted to become a professional student, one of those undisciplined scholars who wanders intermittently from class to class. He read omnivorously and was possessed of a deep passion for writing poetry.

In his many verses we detect more than the romantic nihilism, which was characteristic of disillusioned youth.* In Marx's poetic tragedy entitled *Oulanem,* we read the following

---

* Nihilism is the philosophy of the denial of self, the denial of life. Out of it arises existentialism, the ultimate philosophy of death.

soliloquy by the character who gives his name to the play.

> Ruined, ruined. My time has clean run out.
> The clock has stopped, the pygmy house had crumbled.
> Soon I shall embrace eternity to my breast, and soon
> I shall howl gigantic curses on mankind.
> Ha! Eternity! She is our eternal grief,
> An indescribable and immeasurable Death,
> Vile artificiality conceived to scorn us,
> Ourselves being clockwork, blindly mechanical,
> Made to be the fool-calendars of Time and Space,
> Having no purpose, save to happen, to be ruined,
> So that there shall be something to ruin.
> There had to be some fault in the universe.[61]

As you can well see, that is the Devil speaking. "Ruined, ruined. My time has clean run out." The clock of the cycles of my opportunity to repent and confess that he is Lord has stopped. My time has run out. I am to be ruined because there must be something to ruin.

This is the philosophy of the damned who knew from the moment they were cast out of heaven that if they did not one day repent and be saved, they must pass before the Court of the Sacred Fire and receive the judgment. Those who have failed to confess the incarnate Word in the avatars and in themselves at the end of their evolution pass through the second death.* Marx knew that the second death was awaiting him. And the one who dictated this passage to him, Satan himself, also knew that his own time had come.

The character whose name provides the title of the play is

---

* "But the fearful, and unbelieving, and the abominable, and murderers, and whoremongers, and sorcerers, and idolaters, and all liars, shall have their part in the lake which burneth with fire and brimstone: which is the second death" (Rev. 21:8). The second death is the canceling out of soul identity. It comes as an act of mercy to those souls whose karma is so heavy that the suffering that would be entailed in the balancing of their debt to Life would be too great for any lifestream to bear.

Oulanem, a German traveler, a Mephistophelian character.*
He is Marx as judge and executioner. The word *Oulanem* is an
anagram for Maneluo or Emmanuel, "God with us"—the
Messiah. Marx simply reversed the letters, spelled them back-
wards, and thus he was reversing the name of Christ. This
reversal, this turning around and upside down, is the foundation of the black mass practiced by Satanists.

Lucindo—derived from the Latin *lux*, "light"—is the
companion of Oulanem. Lucindo represents Marx's youthful
intelligence.

Pertini is an Italian citizen and an enemy of Oulanem.
Pertini's name derives from the Latin *perire*, "to perish." He
provides the antithesis for a dialectic struggle never resolved in
the play.

A long first scene ends with the apparent victory of Pertini,
but his last word flung at Lucindo is the German *mistrauen*,
"to mistrust," uttered with seething hatred.

In all of Marx's works there is no comparable passage of
sustained invective. His hatred of the world reaches out to a
vision of world destruction. Oulanem can no longer tolerate
the depravity of men and consigns them to damnation, in a
passage which shows signs of having been written in a single
burst of poetic fury.

Those bursts of fury and creativity that come out of the pit
and out of the Devil are very intense. They are perversions of
the descent of the Holy Ghost upon the sons and daughters of
God. By those bursts of energy, the transfer of the logic of
Satan has been given to the tools of Satan over thousands of
years, and it continues to this very day. You only have to look
at the words that are coming out of punk rock and the overt
Satanism that we have heard in some of the music of acid rock
in the decade of the sixties to realize that these are dictations

---

* In a well-known German legend, Faust is a scholar, bored with the world, who
calls on the Devil to grant him knowledge and magic powers by which to indulge in
worldly pleasure. Mephistopheles is a demon who agrees to serve Faust on the
condition that Faust promises his soul to the Devil.

from devils and demons. And they come in that burst of poetic fury that is being spoken of here.

According to Marx, men do not deserve to live. Therefore, it is time to destroy them utterly. This is the judgment of World Communism: Enter nation by nation and destroy the light-bearers. They do not deserve to live.

Oulanem sees himself as the agent of destruction—not as the destroyer of evil but of Almighty God himself. And since Oulanem cannot destroy Almighty God in his heaven, he will destroy him in his earth, incarnate in his sons and daughters. He is the agent of the destruction of God incarnate, the judge who condemns and then acts as executioner, convinced that he possesses the powers of God to annihilate the universe.

People do not understand this. They have been indoctrinated to believe that God does not live on earth, that he does not live in his sons and daughters. Therefore, they do not perceive that the murder of Almighty God is in fact taking place here on earth every day in the murder of the holy innocents. You say that God cannot be murdered? He is being murdered every day. A misunderstanding of our true theology denies us the real understanding of the theology of the fallen ones.

Oulanem continues, saying that men are no more than apes:

The worlds drag us with them in their rounds,
Howling their songs of death.
And we, we are the apes of a cold God.[62]

There can be no reprieve from this judgment inflicted on mankind, and Oulanem exalts in the prospect of dying when the world dies. He will commit suicide, taking the world with him:

Ha, I must bind myself to a wheel of flame
And dance with joy in the circle of eternity.
If there is something which devours,

I'll leap within it though I bring the world to ruins.
The world that bulks between me and the abyss
I will smash to pieces with my enduring curses.[63]

The Devil has indoctrinated God's children to believe that
they are not God. But think about it: A baby giraffe is a giraffe,
right? A baby porpoise is a porpoise. A baby devil is a devil. A
baby rattlesnake is a rattlesnake. And a child of God is God.
It's very simple. The obvious logic of the Word has always been
simple. That realization is what the fallen ones have taken from
an entire human race, save a tiny percentage who dare to say,
in the face of horrendous condemnation, "I am God."

I was brought up in metaphysics, which has its doctrine
and its dogma, its catechism. You keep reciting it over and over
again until you know your metaphysics. And so I was taught
that I was made in the image and likeness of God,[64] that I was
a reflection of God, but that I was not God, and it would be
blasphemy to think that I was God. It must have been a
thousand times that it went through my mind, "If I am made in
the image and likeness of God, I must be made of the same
essence and substance of which God is made; hence, I am
God." It was clear as crystal.

And yet the catechism would be repeated, "You are only a
reflection of God." Well, if I am only a reflection of God, I
become a robot. If God is looking in the pond and God moves,
then I move too. So what's the point? If I am only a shadow, if
I don't have creativity and free will and cannot move and
rejoice and place upon the altar of God the fruit of my own
cosmic consciousness, which I declare to be his own working
through me, where is the joy of creativity? Where is the joy of
living? Where is the joy of being, if one is but a robot?

A reflection is a robot. Students of metaphysics say they are
a reflection of God. Well, it may be true to a point, but it's not
true to the ultimate point. You were created to be a co-creator
with God, and you cannot get there by being a mere reflection.
You have to be God. And you have to understand what is God.

It is Father, Son, and Holy Spirit as the flame in your heart. It is not your carnal mind. It is not your human consciousness. It is not your human ego, intellect, or desire.

The soul is not the fullness of God. It is God-potential. It is the seed that can become the giant oak tree. That is where humility comes in. It's the proud Satanist who beats upon his breast and says, "I am God." But it is the humble servant son who declares, "Not I, but God in me." And when he says, "Not I," he is denying the human Humpty Dumpty and saying, not the little egg, but the Big Egg. And finally the little egg is swallowed up in the Big Egg, and things equal to the same thing become each other, and you are God incarnate. That is the process of the path of initiation.

Along this path, we encounter those whose soul potential has a far greater and more vast realization of the fullness of God than our own, and therefore we acknowledge them as God-free beings, as the ascended masters. We humbly and lovingly accept the law of hierarchy. We do not demand from the LORD God equal portions of energy and light as that of Elohim, because we know that in the fullness of time and space and evolution, we shall surely become the fullness of Elohim, and until that hour we bow before Elohim.

Another of Marx's poems, "The Player," found its way into a Berlin literary magazine in 1841. It describes a violinist whose delirious frenzy summons the power of darkness.

"Oh player, why playest thou so wild?
Why the savage look in thine eyes?
Why the leaping blood, the soaring waves?
Why tearest thou thy bow to shreds?"

"I play for the sake of the thundering sea
Crashing against the walls of the cliffs,
That my eyes be blinded and my heart burst
And my soul resound in the depths of hell."

"Oh player, why tearest thou thy heart to shreds
In mockery? This art was given thee
By a shining God to elevate the mind
Into the swelling music of the starry dance."

"Look now my blood-dark sword shall stab
Unerringly within thy soul.
God neither knows nor honors art.
The hellish vapors rise and fill the brain,

"Till I go mad and my heart is utterly changed.
See this sword. The prince of darkness sold it to me.
For he beats the time and gives the signs.
Ever more boldly I play the dance of death.

"I must play darkly, I must play lightly,
Until my heart and my violin burst."

The player strikes up on the violin,
His blond hair falling down.
He wears a sword at his side,
And a wide wrinkled gown.[65]

This is the description of a fallen angel, the description of a rock star.

The Religion of Karl Marx

You may be surprised to learn that Karl Marx was not an atheist. In his supposed concern for the exploited masses, Marx was convinced that more was needed than the overthrow of the capitalist bourgeoisie. He writes:

> The abolition of religion as the illusory happiness of man is a demand for their real happiness. The call to abandon their illusions about their conditions is a call to abandon a condition which requires illusions. The criticism of religion is, therefore, the criticism of this vale of tears of which religion is the halo.[66]

Religion is given to us by God as a way to balance our karma. It is a way to bear the burden of the cross and not rebel against that burden. The cross is the symbol of your personal karma that you are given to bear. And when you have borne it through the fourteen stations of the cross and transmuted it, you are given another cross: the cross of planetary karma, the cross of the avatar. Religion teaches us to be long suffering, to endure in love, and to follow love and mercy as the means of transmutation.

Marx's concept of religion as the opium of the people is a flagrant contradiction of facts he knew only too well—historical proof that religion is a most powerful motivating force. Then why was Marx an atheist? Was Marx an atheist? Listen to his own words:

I wish to avenge myself against the one who rules
    above.[67]

Heaven I've forfeited,
I know it full well.
My soul, once true to God,
Is chosen for hell.[68]

That is the full awareness of the archdeceivers of mankind.
They are called the first-class Watchers. They were the top-level
angels who fell with Lucifer and took embodiment, who knew
this principle fully. "My soul, once true to God, is chosen for
hell"—for the second death.

Marx was not an atheist. Marx believed in God and hated
him.

Reverend Richard Wurmbrand says of Marx and his
confreres that "while they openly denounced and reviled God,
they hated a God in whom they believed." His existence is not
challenged; his supremacy is.[69]

The fallen ones have never challenged the existence of God.
They challenge him as the Supreme One. And since they cannot
supplant his supremacy in Spirit, they do so in Matter by a
complicated philosophy. And they have succeeded in dethron-
ing him in the hearts of the vast majority of the evolutions of
earth. These are the facts of the times in which we find
ourselves.

Wurmbrand says:

It might be understood that Communists would
arrest priests and pastors as counter revolutionaries.
But why were priests compelled by the Marxists in the
Romanian prison of Piteshti to say the mass over
excrement and urine? Why were Christians tortured to
take communion with these as the elements? Why the
obscene mockery of religion? Why did the Romanian
Orthodox priest Roman Braga, whom I knew

Richard Wurmbrand (1909–2001) was a Christian minister imprisoned and tortured by the Communist regime in Romania. After his release, he emigrated to America and spent the rest of his life publicizing the fate for Christians who were persecuted for their beliefs.

personally when he was a prisoner of the Communists, and who presently resides in the U.S.A., have his teeth knocked out one by one with an iron rod to make him blaspheme? The Communists had explained to him and others: "If we kill you Christians, you go to heaven. But we don't want you to be crowned martyrs. You should curse God first and then go to hell."[70]

This is going on in the twentieth century in the concentration camps of Russia and Eastern Europe. When there are atrocities that we are not equipped to deal with in the level of the conscious mind but which our subconscious minds are aware of, we like to relegate them to the past. These were past brutalities, past primitivism. They are not happening today.

They are happening today.* We have eyewitness reports from those who have come out of these prisons, notably Richard Wurmbrand, who spent fourteen years in a Romanian

---

* This lecture was delivered in 1978, when persecution and torture of Christians was widespread in Communist nations. It continues today in Communist nations such as China, Cuba, and North Korea as well as in a number of Muslim nations. For current news on the persecution of Christians worldwide, see the website of the organization founded by Richard Wurmbrand, Voice of the Martyrs: www.persecution.com.

prison. He has written many books describing the persecution of Christians. The purpose of this persecution was to extract their victims' light and to force them to deny God. This is because the purpose of World Communism is to destroy the soul and send it to hell.

This is why Jesus told us, "Fear not them who kill the body, but those who destroy the soul in hell." [71] These Christians are the martyrs and the witnesses today who do not fear the destruction of their bodies. They are dying daily, as Paul said,[72] but they are unrelenting and they will not surrender the soul. No matter what the torture, no matter what the brutality, they will never deny the Lord Jesus Christ, and therefore they are indeed "hid with Christ in God."[73]

The Communist persecution of religion can have a human explanation. But the fury of this persecution, beyond any reason, is Satanic.

We have said Marx was not an atheist. Was he a Satanist? Listen to his "Invocation of One in Despair":

> So a God has snatched from me my all
> In the curse and rack of destiny.
> All his worlds are gone beyond recall!
> Nothing but revenge is left to me![74]

Although there is no evidence of Marx's direct involvement with the secretive Satanist church, one of his associates in the First International* was Mikhail Bakunin, a Russian anarchist who wrote, "Satan is the first free-thinker and saviour of the world.... He frees Adam and impresses the seal of humanity and liberty on his forehead by making him disobedient."[75]

Wurmbrand writes:

---

* The First International (1864–1876), also known also as the International Workingmen's Association, was an international organization which sought to unite a variety of left-wing Socialist, Communist, and anarchist political groups. Its first congress was held in 1866 in Geneva.

Mikhail Bakunin (1814–1876), a Russian revolutionary anarchist and an associate of Marx in the First International. Bakunin praised Satan as "the savior of the world."

Bakunin reveals that Proudhon, another major Socialist thinker, and at that time a friend of Karl Marx, also "worshiped Satan."[76] Proudhon in *The Philosophy of Misery* declared that God was the prototype for injustice.[77]

Obviously when you get cast out of God's consciousness, his Spirit, you cry out, "Unjust, unjust."

"We reach knowledge in spite of him, we reach society in spite of him. Every step forward is a victory in which we overcome the Divine."[78]

He exclaims, "God is stupidity and cowardice; God is hypocrisy and falsehood; God is tyranny and poverty; God is evil. Where humanity bows before an altar, humanity, the slave of kings and priests will be condemned.... I swear, God, with my hands stretched out toward the heavens that you are nothing more than an executioner of my reason, the scepter of my conscience."[79]

Pierre-Joseph Proudhon (1809–1865)
According to Bakunin, Proudhon was
the first person to proclaim himself
an anarchist. His writings reveal an
intense anger against God.

In the 1960s, Anton Sandor LaVey wrote *The Satanic Bible* and established his Church of Satan, headquartered in California. Here are a few paragraphs:

> It is a popular misconception that the Satanist does not believe in God. The concept of "God," as interpreted by man, has been so varied throughout the ages, that the Satanist simply accepts the definition which suits him best. Man has always created his gods, rather than his gods creating *him*....
>
> All religions of a spiritual nature are inventions of man. He has created an entire system of gods with nothing more than his carnal brain. Just because he has an ego and cannot accept it, he has had to externalize it into some great spiritual device which he calls "God."...
>
> When all religious faith in lies has waned, it is because man has become closer to himself and farther from "God"; closer to the "Devil." If this is what the devil represents, and a man lives his life in the devil's fane [temple, church], with the sinews of Satan moving his flesh, then he either escapes from the cacklings and

carpings of the righteous, or stands proudly in his secret places of the earth and manipulates the folly-ridden masses through his own Satanic might, until that day when he may come forth in splendor proclaiming, "I AM A SATANIST! BOW DOWN, FOR I AM THE HIGHEST EMBODIMENT OF HUMAN LIFE!"...

Say unto thine own heart, "I am mine own redeemer."

Stop the way of them that would persecute you. Let those who devise thine undoing be hurled back to confusion and infamy. Let them be as chaff before the cyclone and after they have fallen rejoice in thine own salvation.

Then all thy bones shall say pridefully, "Who is like unto me? Have I not been too strong for mine adversaries? Have I not delivered MYSELF by mine own brain and body?"[80]

"I question all things,"[81] LaVey declares. "Doubt everything" is the Marxist creed.[82] "It is only DOUBT which will bring mental emancipation,"[83] agrees LaVey. Thus we see the foundations of Satanism in World Communism.

I have given to you a most brief and condensed exposé. Your own research into this subject will uncover more and more of the same.

The Prophecy

By the Ascended Master Kuthumi

The plan of the false hierarchy is to create a worldwide Church of Satan and a one-world government of Satan in total control of the minds, the souls, and the hearts of mankind. This control is to be gained through the base ignorance of the masses of the people, through their own vulnerability and sensuality, through the fluctuation of their egos, their greed, their lust for power, the pride of the eye, and the desire for manipulation. During the thousand-year period when Satan will remain bound according to the law of the Lord Christ executed by the Four and Twenty Elders, these fallen ones will work feverishly and fiendishly preparing for the return of Satan and his angels, who "shall be loosed out of his prison and shall go out to deceive the nations which are in the four quarters of the earth, Gog and Magog, to gather them together to battle: the number of whom is as the sand of the sea."[84]

The Satanist Church, with its nude female on the altar, its blood rites and black masses, is the diabolical and diametrical opposite of the Church Universal and Triumphant. Seeing the end from the beginning, members of the true Church cannot take lightly their calling or their commitment. They must counter every move of the Satanists in the name of the I AM THAT I AM, as these fallen ones are organized on this and other planets of this solar system on the planes of Mater.

Many contingents of the false hierarchy are preparing for the loosing of Satan and the galvanizing of his legions when they shall go "up on the breadth of the earth and compass the camp of the saints about, and the beloved city."[85] In that day and in that hour, the fire shall come down from God out of heaven to devour them. And the Devil that deceived them will be cast into the lake of fire at the Court of the Sacred Fire on the God Star Sirius where the beast and the false prophet shall already have been taken and have been judged.[86]

Inasmuch as the prophecy of the last judgment and the second death of Satan and his followers is preordained, as was the trial, the judgment, and the second death of Lucifer, it is not with the fate of the fallen ones that we are concerned, but it is with the battle of Armageddon itself, which is waging even now for the souls of the children of God. It is during this thousand-year period that certain of the incarnated fallen angels will be abroad in the earth preaching the philosophy of the Adversary; for during this period the children of God will make their commitment to the right or to the left, for the Real or for the unreal.

Those who confirm the calling of the Christ within in this century will, according to the prophecy given to John the Revelator, "live and reign with Christ a thousand years." These are the souls which John saw who bore witness of Jesus and the Word of God, "which had not worshipped the beast, neither his image, neither had received his mark upon their foreheads or in their hands."[87] But those who fail to make that commitment for Christ and for his true teachings, those who have received the true name of God, I AM THAT I AM, and who have the testimony of the Lord brought forth by the two witnesses, those who have received these gifts and graces of the Spirit yet refuse to be committed to the cause of the true hierarchy, who are half in and half out, the lukewarmed ones, the ones who prefer their selfish existence to the surrender, the sacrifice, and the service of the saints—these will continue to reincarnate until the return of Satan when the choice twixt light and darkness will be the ultimate choice to be or not to be.

At that time and in that space, the children of God who have been trained by the sons and daughters of God in the teachings released by the messengers of the Great White Brotherhood will have to choose between their own carnal mind and their own Christ mind and between Satan and Jesus Christ. Then those who choose God will live forevermore in the I AM THAT I AM and will attain immortality in the ritual of the ascension. The victory over the last enemy, death personified in and as the Devil, will be won.[88]

Then those who choose the carnal mind and Satan will be judged with him before the Court of the Sacred Fire and the Four and Twenty Elders. They shall stand before the "great white throne and him that sat on it, from whose face the earth and the heaven fled away."[89] And they shall see the opening of the Book of Life. Those who choose the carnal mind and Satan will file to the dais where the current of Alpha and Omega is released for either the integration or the disintegration of souls according to the judgments of the Lord. There they will stand with Satan; and in the twinkling of the All-Seeing Eye of God, their souls will be canceled out with his in the ritual of the second death—the highest mercy of the law.

Now let those who realize the momentous work of the millennium understand that the sacrifices of today's light-bearers will determine how many souls are saved and how many are lost in the final judgment of this system of worlds. Those who have been given the sacred trust of the teaching cannot live it halfway; they cannot give of themselves halfway. They cannot be lukewarm, for the Lord God will spue them out of his mouth.[90] And they will not be acceptable as candidates for the ascension....

Now I make known to you a dispensation of the Lords of Karma. If a certain quota of ascensions of Keepers of the Flame is met in this thousand-year period, then in the time appointed for the unloosing of the Devil and his angels, many ascended masters will be given the dispensation to walk the earth in visible light bodies to preach to the mankind of earth who up to that time will have failed to make the choice between light and darkness, Christ and Antichrist, both within the microcosm of self and in the Macrocosm of this solar system.

But if the quota of ascensions is not met, the mankind of earth will have only the inner flame and the voice of God within to confirm their conviction. And in the day of the appearance of Antichrist, the great clamoring of the fallen ones with every form of false-hierarchy teaching will resound from one end of the earth to the other, up until the moment when the angel of the Lord will seize them and bind them and remand them to the Court of the Sacred Fire presided over by the Four and Twenty Elders.[91]

The Choice

You will notice in the Book of Daniel and in the Book of Revelation that there are time periods related. And in the Book of Revelation it is stated, "Satan will be bound for a thousand years and then loosed again."[92] The purpose of this dispensation is that God wants to give his children an opportunity to be free of the aura of Satan, which, when he is present upon earth, fills the entire planetary body. And so God in this century has seen to it that Satan is bound—literally bound behind bars and removed from the earth, whereas Lucifer, the Archdeceiver, has already passed through the second death.[93]

So there is a time in this hour of an intense momentum of light when we are free of the momentum of the darkest of the fallen ones. And this is why light is on the march. This is why there is receptivity to all sorts of New Age teachings and Eastern teachings. These are being taught and received around the world because you do not have the presence of Antichrist through Lucifer and Satan to counteract that search for spirituality in the children of God.

Before these events, which are historical, to say the least, it was practically impossible to even expand the teachings of the ascended masters. Some of you who rejoice to have finally found us wonder why you never heard of us in the last twenty years. It is because during the last twenty years, since the dispensation in 1958 of the publishing of the teachings of Jesus Christ and the ascended masters—during that period Lucifer was abroad in the face of the land, counteracting every action of our messengership, and so, just a nucleus of lightbearers were able to receive the teaching.

I well remember those personal encounters and confrontations and the manner of the binding and the removal of Lucifer which took place after the ascension of our beloved Mark. It was required that he be in the ascended state, in the plane of Spirit and that I be in Matter and that the two witnesses function as the coordinates to give the invocation in Spirit and Matter for the binding of that Fallen One, which binding was performed by Archangel Michael and the many hosts of the Lord. Satan, on the other hand, was bound prior to the ascension of beloved Mark, also by the invocations of our witness.

The giving of the invocation now is up to the sons and daughters of God; the implementation of the invocation is up to the archangels. So we now have the challenge, each one of us, to make the invocation that will bind the power and the seed of Lucifer and Satan in our own temple—namely the carnal mind, the not-self, the synthetic self. Each one of us must stand at the altar of the sacred fire of our own being to challenge what is known as the dweller-on-the-threshold, which is our own carnal mind. It must be slain by the Christ mind. It can only be slain when the soul has surrendered the carnal mind, extricated itself from it, and become one with the Christ mind.

If the carnal mind should be slain by the Christ before the soul has separated itself out from that carnal mind, the soul as well as the carnal mind would be destroyed in the hour of the judgment. That is why the command is given, "Come apart and be a separate people."[94] You have to come apart from those things that are carnally minded in yourself and in your environment and in the community. You have to separate yourself from that which is unreal so that when the unreal goes into the flame, you do not go with it.

That is why we have the teaching. That is why we have the path of initiation. That is why we have the testing on the path. It is all so that we can surrender the human rebellion and the pride and the ego and the lust and the things of this world, so that we in Christ can be a part of the judgment. We must be a part of the judgment because we have free will to accept or reject it.

All of the hosts of the Lord, all of the ascended masters are telling us, "Now is the time to move forward. Now is the hour when the children of light can take over the earth. The Adversary has been bound. You have never had a better opportunity in hundreds of thousands of years to reclaim the earth for the Ancient of Days." So we work while we have the light.

With the conclusion of this thousand-year period, God must unloose Satan and his angels again. God is not going to destroy Satan until the people themselves have rejected him and rejected his vibration in themselves. So they will have a thousand-year period in which to experience what might be called a pre–golden age, the presence of all available light, opportunity, and teaching.

At the conclusion of that period, having been inundated with the teaching and the presence of the ascended masters and their disciples, having truly seen what the light of God is and what it can do, having received the message, heard the teaching, and had access to the books and the gospel preached in every nation, the people must once again face the Adversary. In previous incarnations they failed to challenge him, failed to deny him. They did indeed choose Satan instead of Christ. The ancient cry, "Give us Barabbas,"[95] is the multitude choosing Satan, the carnal mind, rather than choosing Jesus Christ. That same cry echoes across the land today to the shame of this nation. And each time we are dishonest with ourselves, self-deceptive, or deceiving others, we are also saying, "Give us Barabbas." Jesus Christ, as the Christ in our own heart, is crucified afresh each time we choose the not-self.[96]

The period known as a thousand years is to me the enigma of God. God speaks in the Bible in terms of "a time, and times, and a half a time." He speaks in terms of "a thousand years."[97] But to God these are cycles, and we have the ancient teaching that is a key to the deciphering of these time periods.

Many God-fearing people really desire to know the interpretation of the end times through the Book of Daniel, through the prophets, through Jesus (Matthew 24 and Luke 21), and also through the Book of Revelation, and they have devised all sorts of systems to decipher these prophecies. But the real key to understanding epochs and eras and cycles in the Bible is very simple: "One day is with the Lord as a thousand years, and a thousand years as one day,"[98] and "Except those days should be shortened, no flesh should be saved, but for the elect's sake, those days shall be shortened."[99] *Days* means "cycles"—cycles of consciousness.

The final interpretation of time and space is, "In the twinkling of an eye, the last trump will sound, and death will be swallowed up in victory."[100] A thousand years may be the twinkling of the eye of God. It may be a day, it may be a century, it may be a month, it may be ten years. We cannot limit ourselves to seeing it as a thousand years as we measure time.

The beloved city referred to in the Book of Revelation is the New Jerusalem, and the focus of that city is right here in Los Angeles. We know that here is the warfare between good and evil; here is where good and evil are in confrontation. And this city is the archetype of all cities.

The pattern repeats itself through the chakras of the nations again and again. And so everyone must look upon his own city, his own community, as the City Foursquare. He must see that community, that time and space, as the place where he must conquer through Christ, and light must swallow up darkness.

Mother's Manifesto

This message that I have given to you is only a part of the exposure of the fundamentals of World Communism—the ancient lie modernized through *The Communist Manifesto* and through the subsequent work of Lenin, Stalin, and others. The Karmic Board has called for the writing of *Mother's Manifesto* as the manifesto that would expose and destroy the manifesto of the fallen ones set forth by Marx and Engels. The writing of this manifesto is truly the challenge of my life and of our lives together.

You can see that the lie is so complex that it involves the entire sequence of events not only in this planetary body but in this system of worlds. *Mother's Manifesto* is the document of divine truth that declares who you really are in God. In other words, it sets forth the truth of the science of being as its premise, as its thesis. And then it takes the sword of living truth and it cleaves asunder the Real from the unreal in this crisscrossing of the threads of light and darkness that the fallen ones have used to gain acceptance for the lie.

The lie itself is, "We have determined to destroy the human race. We have determined to destroy God incarnate. We have determined to destroy the path of initiation and of the ascension in the light. We have come to murder God on earth."

That lie cannot be stated so coldly. It would be totally unacceptable. So it is stated by the most complex systems of rationalization. The false doctrine and false dogma of the fallen ones is not limited to religion or to speculative philosophy or theology. People are always looking for the false Christs and the false prophets in the religions of the world. They have appeared there, but they are far more powerful in the governments, in the economies, in science, and in education. They have long ago destroyed the religions of the world as having the fullness of truth. The fallen ones have long ago determined that their position of power, manipulation, mechanization, and control should be right where it rests today, in what I have called the International Capitalist/ Communist Conspiracy.

You may wonder why I haven't mentioned the Big Lie that has infiltrated World Capitalism. It is simply because I cannot thoroughly examine this error all at once. I must take it systematically and scientifically. I must leave no stone unturned. I must leave no doubt and fear in the hearts of the children of God. And by the time we have finished, we will have the full statement.

And once we have the full statement, do not think that the job is finished. That's when the job begins, because the world is not converted by books. Books are a record and a statement of truth for lightbearers. You eat the book up. It's sweet in the mouth; it's bitter in the belly.[101] You become the book and you go out. And the world is saved by only one process—the conversion of the Holy Ghost.

So we are writing *Mother's Manifesto* together. And it is truly in the name of the Father and of the Son and of the Holy Spirit that it is done, it is finished, and it will be sealed.

Notes

1. "He saith unto them, But whom say ye that I am? And Simon Peter answered and said, Thou art the Christ, the Son of the living God. And Jesus answered and said unto him, Blessed art thou, Simon Barjona: for flesh and blood hath not revealed it unto thee, but my Father which is in heaven. And I say also unto thee, That thou art Peter, and upon this rock I will build my church; and the gates of hell shall not prevail against it" (Matt. 16:15–18).
2. Rev. 1:8, 11; 21:6; 22:13.
3. "And the dragon stood before the woman which was ready to be delivered, for to devour her child as soon as it was born" (Rev. 12:14).
4. In 1978, the time of this lecture, the white-minority government of Rhodesia (now known as Zimbabwe) was fighting against Marxist guerilla forces backed by the Soviet Union and Communist China. Under the pressure of international sanctions, the government agreed to hold elections in 1980, which were won by Robert Mugabe, leader of the largest insurgent group, ZANU-PF. Since that time, Mugabe's Socialist policies have led to the economic ruination of what was formerly one of the wealthiest nations of Africa.

   In 1975, when Cambodia was taken over by the Khmer Rouge, the regime embarked on a program to radically remake society into a Communist utopia. They killed hundreds of thousands of political opponents and racial minorities, and inspired by Mao's Communist China, forced the entire population of major cities to march to rural areas to work on agricultural collectives. Although there is no way of accurately counting, it is estimated that as many as three to four million Cambodians out of a population of some seven million were murdered or died from disease, malnutrition, or forced labor during the four-year Khmer Rouge regime. See John Barron and Anthony Paul, *Murder of a Gentle Land* (New York: Reader's Digest Press, 1977).
5. The City Foursquare described in the Book of Revelation is the New

Jerusalem, archetype of golden-age, etheric cities of light that exist even now on the etheric plane (in heaven) and are waiting to be lowered into physical manifestation (on earth). In order that this vision and prophecy be fulfilled, Jesus taught us to pray with the authority of the spoken Word, "Thy kingdom come on earth as it is in heaven!" Metaphysically speaking, the City Foursquare is the mandala of the four planes and the quadrants of the Matter universe, the four sides of the Great Pyramid of Christ's consciousness focused in the Matter spheres. The twelve gates are gates of Christ's consciousness marking the lines and the degrees of the initiations he has prepared for his disciples.

6. James 1:22.

7. Matt. 11:30.

8. One way in which central banks increase the money supply is through lending money that they create out of nothing. The Federal Reserve also creates money out of nothing through "quantitative easing," the purchase of government bonds, which are then a debt owed to the Fed. When the amount of money increases in this way, the value of that money will decrease proportionally, which is known as inflation. Continual increases in the money supply are the reason why it takes about twenty-four dollars in 2019-money to purchase what would have cost one dollar in 1913, the year the Federal Reserve system was created.

9. 1 Cor. 3:6.

10. On October 20, 1987, Elizabeth Clare Prophet explained that in the early golden ages of this planet and other systems of worlds, the divine spark, the threefold flame, was once "fully the height that we are [today].... The flame was reduced because of mankind's misuse of the light.... You remember the words that are recorded in Genesis that before the Flood, which was the sinking of Atlantis, people lived to be 900 years old, and after that the lifespan was reduced to threescore and ten. Since our life depends upon the divine spark, so the reduction in the divine spark resulted in the reduction of the crystal cord and the lifespan."

11. Matt. 11:12.

12. Cain and Abel, sons of Adam and Eve, brought offerings to the LORD. Abel, who was a keeper of sheep, brought a burnt offering from the firstlings of his flock, while Cain, a tiller of the ground, offered fruit. When Abel's sacrifice was found acceptable and Cain's was rejected, Cain was very wroth. And the LORD said unto him, "Why art thou wroth.... If thou doest well, shalt thou not be

accepted? and if thou doest not well, sin lieth at the door." Cain then slew his brother (Gen. 4:1–8).

13. 1 Cor. 12:3.
14. Gen. 3:16.
15. Gen. 3:19.
16. This initiation is also described in 1 Corinthians, chapter 3. "The fire shall try every man's work of what sort it is. If any man's work abide which he hath built thereupon, he shall receive a reward. If any man's work shall be burned, he shall suffer loss: but he himself shall be saved; yet so as by fire."
17. Gen. 19:17–26.
18. Matt. 25:40.
19. "After those days, saith the LORD, I will put my law in their inward parts, and write it in their hearts; and will be their God, and they shall be my people" (Jer. 31:33).
20. See Rev. 2:11; 20:6, 11–15; 21:7, 8.
21. Gen. 28:10–19.
22. Heb. 7:2–3.
23. Under the guise of combating racism, the World Council of Churches and the United Methodist Church gave millions of dollars to Marxist groups in Africa and Central America that had the aim of overthrowing elected governments and installing Marxist dictatorships. See "Church Group's Aid to Rhodesian Rebels Widely Assailed," *Washington Post*, 18 August 1978, p. A21; Joseph A. Harriss, "Which Master Is the World Council of Churches Serving ... Karl Marx or Jesus Christ?" *Reader's Digest*, August 1982, pp. 130–34; "CBS Hits the Councils of Churches," *AIM Report*, February-B, 1983.
24. One example of America giving millions to support corrupt leaders is Mobutu Sese Seko, ruler of Zaire (now Democratic Republic of the Congo) from 1965 to 1997. The nation was one of the largest recipients of U.S. aid to Africa, even though the regime was notorious for its corruption. During his rule, it is estimated that Mobutu embezzled an estimated $5 billion from the nation. He was known for such extravagances as chartering the Concorde for shopping trips to Paris while the nation's infrastructure crumbled and his people died from starvation and illness.
25. For example, the Peace Corps, established by John F. Kennedy March 1, 1961.
26. Gen. 18:32.
27. "We are the children of God: and if children, then heirs; heirs of

God, and joint-heirs with Christ" (Romans 8:16–17).

28. For more on the persecution of Christians in Communist nations, see pages 134–35.

29. For one account of these events, see the early Christian text *Vitae Adae et Evae*, chapters 11 to 16.

30. Rev. 12:7–9.

31. Matt. 12:30–32; Mark 3:28–30; Luke 12:8–10.

32. Dan. 9:27, 11:31, 12:11; Matt. 24:15; Mark 13:14.

33. Rev. 12:1.

34. Rom. 12:9.

35. Rev. 5:9; 14:3.

36. Gen. 1:26, 28, 31; 2:15–17.

37. Gen. 3:1–6.

38. Matt. 4:8–9.

39. Gen. 3:6.

40. Matt. 13:24–30.

41. Matt. 7:16, 20.

42. No precise enumeration of the number of deaths worldwide caused by Communism since 1917 is possible. This is the result of the loss of (or inability to keep) records due to civil war, state-organized famines, forced relocations, collectivization, terror, political executions, disease, malnutrition and the general hardship that accompanies the takeover and process of consolidating power by the Communists—and the suppression of such information as a matter of state policy. Nevertheless, eyewitness accounts, demographic information, and such historical records that have survived enabled scholars to estimate at least 190 million deaths due to Communism up to 1986. These include the Soviet Union, 110 million dead (Alexander Solzhenitsyn, *Warning to the West*, p. 129); China, 64 million (*The Human Cost of Communism in China*, p. iv); Cambodia, 4 million killed by Khmer Rouge (*Current Biography*, 1980, s.v. "Pol Pot"); Afghanistan, 2 million (Jan Goodwin, *Caught in the Crossfire*, p. 21); Vietnam, 1.4 million (Guenter Lewy, *America in Vietnam*, p. 453, and *Los Angeles Times*, 1 May 1985, sec. 2); Korea, 4 million (Lewy, p. 450); Poland, 1.2 million (*Encyclopaedia Britannica*, 15th ed., s.v. "Poland, History of"); Ethiopia, 1.1 million (*New American*, 17 February 1986, p. 18, and *Insight*, 4 August 1986, p. 4); Mozambique, 175,000 (*New American*, 2 March 1987, p. 21, and internal memorandum of the Office of U.S. Foreign Disaster Assistance, 28 December 1986); Angola, 70,000 (*Human Events*, 19 August 1978, p. 11); Hungary, 32,000 (*World*

Almanac and Book of Facts, 1987, p. 578); El Salvador, 50,000 (Interview with Alejandro Bolaños of the Nicaraguan Information Center, 13 June 1987); Nicaragua, 30,000 (Interview with Alejandro Bolaños); South Yemen, 12,000 (*Time*, 3 February 1986, p. 43). The total thus far is 188 million deaths. Additional deaths have occurred in the Soviet Union since 1959, in Cambodia (before and after Pol Pot), in China since 1970, in East Germany, Czechoslovakia, Yugoslavia, Romania, the Baltic Republics, Cuba, Zimbabwe, and at the hands of Communist guerrilla movements around the world.

43. Pythagoras (570–495 BC) founded his mystery school in 530 BC at Crotona in southern Italy. Here, carefully selected men and women pursued a philosophy based upon the mathematical expression of universal law, illustrated in music and in the rhythm and harmony of a highly disciplined way of life. After a five-year probation of strict silence, Pythagorean students progressed through a series of initiations whereby the son or daughter of God may become, as Pythagoras' *Golden Verses* state, "a deathless God divine, mortal no more."

44. Matt. 19:17; Mark 10:18; Luke 18: 19.

45. Rom. 13:8–10.

46. Francis Wheen, *Karl Marx: A Life* (New York: Norton, 2001), p. 22.

47. August Thalheimer, *Introduction to Dialectical Materialism: The Marxist Worldview* (Covici Friede, 1935), part 7, "Hegel and Feuerbach." Available online at www.marxists.org/archive/thalheimer/works/dimat/07.htm.

48. Thalheimer summarizing Feuerback's philosophy in *Introduction to Dialectical Materialism*.

49. Ludwig Feuerbach, *The Essence of Christianity* (London: Kegan Paul, 1890), ch. 16.

50. For a more detailed introduction to Feuerbach's philosophy, see Stanford Encyclopedia of Philosophy online, s.v. "Ludwig Andreas Feuerbach." https://plato.stanford.edu/entries/ludwig-feuerbach/

51. Karl Marx, quoted in Isaiah Berlin, *Karl Marx: His Life and Environment* (New York: Oxford University Press, 1996), p. 53.

52. Isa. 55:11.

53. "The history of all hitherto existing society is the history of class struggles." *The Manifesto of the Communist Party* (1848), sect. 1, para. 1.

54. Rom. 3:8.

55. When addressing Western ambassadors at a reception at the Polish Embassy in Moscow, on November 18, 1956, Soviet Premier Nikita Khrushchev said, "Whether you like it or not, history is on our side. We will bury you!" Many Americans interpreted Kruschev's statement as a threat of nuclear war, but it was actually based on his belief in Marx's theory that a Socialist society was the inevitable goal of human history.

56. See Part 1 of this book for an explanation of the foundation of the free-enterprise system in Jesus' parable of the talents.

57. See Sanat Kumara, *The Opening of the Seventh Seal* (Gardiner, Mont.: The Summit Lighthouse Library, 2001), chapter 2.

58. 2 Tim. 3:7.

59. 1 Cor. 15:53.

60. 1 Cor. 15:50.

61. Karl Marx, *Oulanem*, act 1, scene 3, quoted in Richard Wurmbrand, *Was Karl Marx a Satanist?* (Diane Books, 1979), p. 13, 14.

62. *Oulanem*, act 1, scene 3.

63. Ibid.

64. Gen. 1:26.

65. Robert Payne, *The Unknown Karl Marx* (New York: New York University Press, 1971), pp. 59–60.

66. Karl Marx, *Critique of Hegel's "Philosophy of Right,"* Introduction, quoted in Richard Wurmbrand, *Marx and Satan* (Westchester, Ill.: Crossway Books, 1986), p. 10.

67. Karl Marx, "Invocation of One in Despair," quoted in Wurmbrand, *Marx and Satan*, p. 12.

68. Karl Marx, "The Pale Maiden," quoted in Wurmbrand, *Marx and Satan*, p. 22.

69. Wurmbrand, *Marx and Satan*, p. 29 (emphasis in original).

70. Richard Wurmbrand, *Marx: Prophet of Darkness* (Basingstoke, UK: Marshall Pickering, 1986), pp. 64–65.

71. Matt. 10:28.

72. 1 Cor. 15:31.

73. Col. 3:3.

74. Wurmbrand, *Marx: Prophet of Darkness*, p. 10.

75. Mikhail Bakunin, *God and the State*.

76. Hans Enzensberger, *Gespäche mit Marx und Engels (Conversations with Marx and Engels)* (Frankfurt-am-Main: Insel Verlag, 1973), p. 17.

77. Wurmbrand, *Marx: Prophet of Darkness*, p. 23.

78. Pierre-Joseph Proudhon, *Philosophie de la Misère (The Philosophy*

of Misery) (Paris: Union Général d'Editions, 1964), pp. 199–200.

79. Ibid., pp. 200–201; Wurmbrand, *Marx: Prophet of Darkness*, pp. 23–24.

80. Anton Szandor LaVey, *The Satanic Bible* (New York: Avon Books, 1969), pp. 40, 44, 45, 33–34.

81. Ibid., p. 31.

82. Asked for his favorite epigram, Marx responded, *de omnibus disputandum*, "doubt everything." www.marxists.org/archive/marx/works/1865/04/01.htm

83. LaVey, *Satanic Bible*, p. 39.

84. Rev. 20:7–8.

85. Rev. 20:9.

86. Rev. 20: 9–10.

87. Rev. 20:4.

88. 1 Cor. 15:26.

89. Rev. 20:11.

90. Rev. 3:16.

91. Kuthumi, "An Exposé of False Teachings," XV, *Pearls of Wisdom*, vol. 19, no. 15, April 11, 1976.

92. Rev. 20:1–3.

93. Lucifer went through the final judgment and second death on April 26, 1975. See Elizabeth Clare Prophet, *The Great White Brotherhood in the Culture, History, and Religion of America* (Gardiner, Mont.: Summit University Press, 2004), ch. 19.

94. Exod. 33:16; Lev. 20:24, 26; 2 Cor. 6:17.

95. Matt. 27:21; Mark15:11; Luke 3:18; John 18:39–40.

96. Heb. 6:6.

97. Rev. 12:14; 20:2–7.

98. 2 Pet. 3:8; Ps. 90:4.

99. Matt. 24:22.

100. 1 Cor. 15:52, 54 (paraphrased).

101. Ezek. 3:1–3; Rev. 10:8–11.

www.ingramcontent.com/pod-product-compliance
Lightning Source LLC
Chambersburg PA
CBHW052007090426
42741CB00008B/1590